Teaching for Learning
Mathematics

Teaching for Learning Mathematics

Rosamund Sutherland

 Open University Press

Open University Press
McGraw-Hill Education
McGraw-Hill House
Shoppenhangers Road
Maidenhead
Berkshire
England
SL6 2QL

email: enquiries@openup.co.uk
world wide web: www.openup.co.uk

and Two Penn Plaza, New York, NY 10121–2289, USA

First published 2007

A catalogue record of this book is available from the British Library

ISBN-10: 0 335 21390 1 (pb), 0 335 21391 X (hb)
ISBN-13: 978 0 335 21390 0 (pb), 978 0 335 21391 7 (hb)

Library of Congress Cataloguing-in-Publication Data
CIP data applied for

Typeset by YHT Ltd, London
Printed in the UK by Bell & Bain Ltd, Glasgow

The **McGraw·Hill** Companies

Contents

Acknowledgements

I am indebted to all my colleagues in the Graduate School of Education at the University of Bristol for providing me with the intellectual stimulus which has enabled me to write this book. Guy Claxton, Andrew Pollard, John Furlong and Martin Hughes have pushed me to think beyond the frame of mathematics education. Laurinda Brown has been a critical friend who has continuously questioned my assumptions about teaching and learning mathematics, as have all the doctoral students I have worked with, and in particular Federica Olivero. It has been a great pleasure working within the international mathematics education community and I especially want to thank Teresa Rojano and Nicolas Balacheff who have so productively argued with me over the years.

I would like to thank my parents, Joan Reynolds and Percy Hatfield, who experienced the transformative potential of education, in which I so passionately believe. Also my close family, Ian, Joanna and Andrew who always give me the strength to believe in my work as an academic.

Finally I would like to thank Mary O'Connell who steadfastly supports all of my endeavours and without whose support I could not have finished this book.

1 Teaching, Learning and Mathematics

Opening remarks

> Children can say more than they realize and it is through coming to understand what is meant by what is said that their cognitive skills develop.
>
> (Wertsch and Stone 1985:167)

Young people learn mathematics at school to educate them in some way for life outside school. This education has many possible purposes. It could be about learning to become an informed citizen. It could be about learning to appreciate the ways in which mathematics plays an increasingly important 'hidden' role in the life of the twenty-first century, for example in the growing computer games industry. It could be about education for the world of work. It could be about education for higher education after school. Or it could be about education for everyday life. These possible purposes relate to different mathematical practices, different ways of knowing mathematics, different mathematical objects, technologies and symbols and different ways of being empowered by mathematics.

Whatever the reason almost every young person in the world has to learn mathematics in school. Yet for many this is a difficult and increasingly disengaging experience. Why is this the case and can anything be done about it? What can we learn from mathematics lessons in which students are engaged and motivated to struggle with difficult mathematical ideas? What can we learn from research on teaching and learning mathematics? This book aims to address these questions and has been written for all those teachers, researchers and policy makers who want to encourage young people to become engaged with and learn mathematics.

Research-informed practice

Mathematics education research is a strong and developing area which draws from fields such as psychology, sociology, cognitive science and philosophy. There is an enormous literature on learning mathematics which could be of value to teachers and policy makers.[1] However, most teachers are unaware of the literature and many would find it inaccessible, overly fragmented and confusing in the multiple messages which it conveys.

How then can a teacher begin to make sense of the research which is available? This is a question which I asked myself many years ago when I was first faced with teaching negative numbers to a class of 12-year-old students. None of the teachers in the school where I was teaching appeared to be interested in my questions and I soon learned to stop asking them. Eventually I moved to teaching mathematics in a further education college and studied for a Certificate in Education at the local polytechnic.[2] Although the course I was studying gave me access to new ways of thinking about teaching in general, it never came close to considering issues related to teaching and learning mathematics. And so finally after five years of teaching I decided to become a researcher in mathematics education, motivated by a desire to ask questions and by not having found a community within schools and colleges which seemed interested in the questions I was asking. It was only then that I began to realize that there was already a large research literature available which I could have drawn upon. I discovered national and international mathematics education research communities which had been struggling for years over similar questions to those which had been troubling me. And I began to learn from these communities.

I suspect that many mathematics teachers still experience what I experienced as a young teacher. They do not know where to find the communities and literature which could support their questioning about teaching and learning mathematics. They are then likely to stop asking questions, unless as in my case they move into a research community. This is unfortunate because questioning and inquiry are at the heart of all learning. And non-questioning teachers are likely to lead to non-questioning students. And non-questioning students are missing out on opportunities to become actively engaged in their own learning. And even more worryingly, a research community which is more or less cut off from a teaching community is not likely to produce research which will be valued or used by teachers.

This book presents alternatives to this divided and often divisive model of research and teaching and argues for new communities to be developed which will enable researchers and teachers to work in partnership on the construction of knowledge for teaching and learning mathematics.

Theory as a way of seeing

The word theory in its original sense means 'to see' and as Davis et al. (2000: 52) point out: 'Humans are irrepressible theorisers. We can't help but note similarities among diverse experiences, to see relationships among events, and to develop theories that explain these relationships (and that predict others)'. This irrepressible theorizing leads teachers to develop informal theories about teaching and learning which inevitably influence their teaching practices. This is because theories influence what we see. For example, if a teacher implicitly believes in a concept of mathematical ability then he or she is likely to interpret differences in students' mathematical attainment as being caused by differences in 'ability'. This in its turn is likely to influence students' views about themselves and their potential for learning mathematics.

In a similar way researchers develop informal theories which influence their research practices. When I first started researching the relationship between Logo programming and learning mathematics[3] I wrote field notes as I observed students working together at the computer. I also video recorded students' interactions with the computer. When I began to analyse the video recordings I realized how my field notes had been implicitly influenced by my existing theories of teaching and learning. Influenced by the prevailing constructivist theory of learning,[4] I thought that the teacher's role would be minimal and so I did not pay much attention to this role As I began to transcribe the video recordings of students' work I began to realize how wrong this assumption was. I knew from this time that the teacher's role was crucial and over the years have developed a theoretical perspective which reflects this point of view. In some ways this book tells the story of this evolving perspective and how this relates to the development of new ways of researching in mathematics education.

If teachers and researchers are irrepressible theorizers, so also are students. In the mathematics classroom students develop informal theories which relate to what they see and their previous history of learning. For example, 10–11-year-old primary school students when asked to write down what they noticed about a parallelogram wrote: 'It has four sides; they are like train tracks; they are parallel; all sides are equal; it doesn't have any right angles; it's the colour turquoise; it can be a diamond'.[5] All of these statements are correct in the context of what the students actually observed but some are more mathematically appropriate than others. The 10–11-year-old students were working within a computer-based environment which had been designed to introduce them to the properties of quadrilaterals (to be discussed more extensively in Chapter 8). Unthinkingly this environment had been designed so that parallelograms were always the colour turquoise, and so students began to generalize about this property. Parallel lines 'as train tracks' was an idea introduced to them by their teacher in a previous lesson, an idea which had possibly been helpful as a way into the idea of parallel lines, but became less helpful as they increasingly met parallel lines which did not look to them like 'train tracks', because they were too far apart.

It is important for teachers, researchers and students to find ways of making their theories visible, putting them on the table, as it were, for discussion and refinement. This involves becoming part of a community in which emerging theories are discussed, confronted and developed.

Researchers are already part of a 'scientific' community who exchange and debate their ideas about teaching and learning mathematics. But teachers are usually not part of such a 'scientific' community. With notable exceptions (for example in Japan[6]) teachers tend to work in isolation in their schools, very rarely engaging with other teachers or with the mathematics education research community. Within this book I argue for teachers and researchers to become part of a wider community in which theories about teaching and learning are discussed, confronted and modified. I also argue for teachers and researchers to work together in this theory-building process. In this way theory can become a tool for thinking about teaching and learning mathematics. I return to these issues in Chapters 7, 9 and 10.

Mathematics students can also become part of a scientific community in which mathematical theories are made visible, constructed and confronted. Such a classroom community could be called a 'community of inquiry' and involves a teacher working with students in ways which value both the students' own theories and mathematical theories which have been developed over centuries. These ideas are discussed in detail in Chapters 3, 4 and 5.

A socio-cultural perspective

There are many possible theoretical perspectives which could inform teaching and learning mathematics.[7] This book mainly draws on a socio-cultural perspective. This approach emphasizes the social and cultural contexts of learning, emphazing the mediating role of people in this process. It also centres around the idea that all human activity is mediated by technologies and tools which have been invented by people within a particular cultural context.

Chapter 2 focuses on the 'cultures of mathematics education' which frame what teachers and students 'can do' in the classroom. This includes a discussion of how what a teacher 'can do' in the classroom is structured by a particular school culture, a particular curriculum culture and a particular assessment culture, and how these differ from country to country. It also includes a discussion of the similarities and differences between the mathematical tools which are privileged in different countries. For example, in Hong Kong (and other Pacific Rim countries) there is a resurgence of interest in the abacus as a tool for doing mathematics. In the USA and the UK there is questioning of the role of the calculator in primary mathematics classrooms. I will argue in Chapter 2 that awareness and understanding of these multiple influences enable them to be used as structuring resources, as liberating as opposed to confining constraints.[8]

Socio-cultural theory emphasizes the fact that students actively construct knowledge drawing on what they already know and believe.[9] From this perspective students bring informal perspectives on mathematics to any new learning situation and these influence what they pay attention to and thus the knowledge they construct. Chapter 3 centres around a discussion of these informal perspectives and argues that whereas it is important for teachers to be aware of and draw upon such perspectives, these may not spontaneously evolve into the more formal mathematical approaches which are usually the focus of school learning. For example, trial-and-error approaches to solving equations do not spontaneously evolve into algebraic approaches. Empirical approaches to justifying a conjecture in mathematics do not spontaneously evolve into mathematical proof. Repeated addition does not spontaneously evolve into multiplication. However, if as teachers we learn to pay attention to these informal approaches, we can use them as a basis for learning powerful new mathematical ideas.

Mathematical tools

Over the centuries mathematicians have invented new 'mathematical' tools which support mathematical activity. These invented tools include material tools, such as the ruler, the abacus and the calculator. They also include symbolic tools, such as the Cartesian coordinate system and the long multiplication algorithm. Studying the history of an invented tool will always show that the particular invented tool emerged from a cultural context in which there was a pragmatic need for such a tool. For example, in the third century the Chinese developed a system of negative numbers for solving problems such as:

> By selling 2 cows and 5 goats to buy 13 pigs, there is a surplus of 1000 cash. The money obtained from selling 3 cows and 3 pigs is just enough to buy 9 goats. By selling 6 goats and 8 pigs to buy 5 cows, there is a deficit of 600 cash. What is the price of a cow, a goat and a pig?

Interestingly material objects – counting rods – were used to represent negative numbers. Sometimes different coloured rods were used, for example red to represent a surplus and black to represent a deficit. This is a powerful example of the mathematical concept being inextricably linked to the set of problems to be solved and the material objects (tools) and language development for this purpose.[10]

Tools have also been invented specifically for teaching and learning mathematics, for example the symbolic number line[11] and material artefacts such as Dienes blocks.[12] These tools are usually intended to scaffold the path towards the learning of particular mathematical ideas. In Chapter 9 I discuss why such pedagogic tools are qualitatively different from the mathematical tools discussed earlier, and need to be understood as such. Mathematicians and mathematics educators also use more general purpose tools such as paper and pencil, word processors and books, and the worldwide web. These tools are used both as a means of communicating mathematical ideas and a source of mathematical knowledge.

Socio-cultural theory suggests that the use of a particular tool potentially transforms what a person can do. This is the 'big idea' behind this book. For example, algebra potentially transforms the range of mathematical problems which can be solved. This relatively straightforward yet powerful idea, which is inherent in the emergence of new tools, is not so evident in the mathematics classroom. Instead most students view algebra (for example) as a confusing new tool which can become a barrier to their enjoyment of mathematics.

Each tool allows us to do different things, produce different mathematics. The long multiplication algorithm enables people to perform calculations on paper which would be almost impossible to carry out mentally. Such paper-and-pencil algorithmic tools are controversial because there is a tendency nowadays to think that with the advent of computers people no longer need to know how to perform such algorithms on paper. In the history of the development of mathematics many such algorithmic tools have become extinct as new tools were invented, for example the algorithm for calculating square roots. From the perspective of mathematics education it is important to analyse what a particular tool privileges or potentially enables a person to do and the potential purpose of each tool for learning and doing mathematics (to be discussed more fully in Chapter 9).

Focusing on mathematical tools is not usually how mathematicians and mathematics educators think about mathematics. For most mathematicians mathematics is associated with mental work, which is often accompanied by a denial of the use of even such traditional tools as paper and pencil. Even when mathematicians use tools, such as paper, books and mathematical conversation, they do not tend to acknowledge the role of these resources in learning and producing mathematics. The culture of being a mathematician (at least a 'pure' mathematician) is associated with the enlightenment tradition of the scientist working alone. However, even mental mathematical work involves visualizing mathematical tools. There is evidence, for example, that Chinese students who have learned to use a 'concrete' abacus visualize this concrete tool when calculating mentally.[13]

In the worlds outside 'pure mathematics' it is clear that people make extensive use of both digital and non-digital tools when they are engaged in mathematical-related problem solving. Carpenters in the building trade carry out calculations on as-yet-undecorated plaster. Engineers calculate on the backs of envelopes. Accountants make extensive use of the digital spreadsheet. Applied mathematicians use computer programming packages such as Maple.[14] I argue throughout this book that resourceful learners (whether teachers or students) are people who are aware of the range of tools which they can draw upon within a particular situation – when for example to use a digital tool such as a graph-plotting package and when to use a paper-and-pencil graph.

In mathematics digital tools do not necessarily replace non-digital tools. I sometimes find myself using a long division algorithm when working out what each person has to pay when sharing a bill in a restaurant. I use a spreadsheet to construct budgets. I use my fingers when working out which is the month in six months' time. I use tallies when making rapid counts of numbers of people in particular categories. I have used a graph to work out when the Christmas turkey will be cooked (by plotting temperature against time). I have never been particularly good at memorizing mathematical facts (or indeed at memorizing anything) and learned to deduce formulae from first principles. In this sense I learned to use theory as a tool to help me remember mathematics (for example, the rule for finding the roots of a quadratic equation and the rule for finding the sum of an arithmetic series). This idea of theory as a tool will be developed further in Chapter 9.

Teaching and learning mathematics

One of the aims of this book is to focus on the interrelationship between teaching and learning mathematics, with the emphasis being on interrelationship. A focus on learning alone tends to ignore the role of the teacher and a focus on teaching alone tends to ignore the diversity of students' learning. In Russian the word *'obuchenie'* means the interaction of teachers and students.[15] In Japanese the word *'taushushido'* conjoins teaching and learning. In France the phrase *'didactiques des mathematiques'* mean the interrelationship between teaching, learning and mathematics. It seems that it is only in the English-speaking world that there is no word which links together the practice of teaching and learning. As Clarke (2002: 6) has pointed out:

> other communities have acknowledged the interdependence of instruction and learning by encompassing both activities within the same process, and most significantly within the same word. The existence of such a term in English would transform our interpretation of the activities of the classroom and encourage (or compel) us to identify communal practices and the progressive participation in a common discourse as essential features, rather than fragmenting the

classroom into teaching and learning activities undertaken by individuals.

Understanding these differences in words and meaning also throws light on the very different approaches to researching teaching and learning in different countries. It is quite possible that English-speaking countries have historically separated research on teaching from research on learning because there is no word which brings together the two concepts.

So what word can we use in English-speaking countries? The word 'didactics' has become associated, for English-speaking people, with overly prescriptive ways of teaching – 'tending to give instruction or advice, even when it is not welcome or not needed'.[16] Another possible word is 'pedagogy', but this word has become over-associated with the idea of teaching strategies, separated from learning and also separated from mathematics. Clarke (2002) has chosen to use the phrase 'instructed learning' which points to a relationship between teaching and learning. However, this phrase loses the important link to mathematics and the word 'instruction' also has connotations of 'direction'.

The whole thrust of this book is on the inextricable relationships between mathematics and teaching and learning. So, despite the cumbersome nature of the phase, 'teaching and learning mathematics' is what I have chosen to use throughout this book. More importantly I have chosen the title of the book to be *Teaching for Learning Mathematics*. This is because teaching does not always seem to pay attention to learning. In Chapter 5 I begin to disentangle the complex processes of teaching and learning mathematics, discussing the importance of making learning visible in the mathematics classroom.

Designing for learning

There seems to be a myth that exceptional students are able to learn mathematics almost effortlessly through their own interest, inquiry and endeavour. This myth works against the needs of the vast majority of students. The vast majority of young people begin to access more formal mathematical ideas when they are part of a 'mathematical' community, where mathematics is self-consciously practised. The vast majority of young people are unlikely to find such communities outside school. This is why schooling is still so important in the twenty-first century. This is a rather unfashionable notion among many educationalists who believe that schools are outdated and archaic institutions. I am not suggesting that schools do not have to change, but that we need to understand more fully the conditions which engender mathematics learning before engaging in radical reform.

However schools are reconfigured, I suggest that mathematics teachers will always have an important role in that 'appropriately arranged contrasts can help people notice new features that previously escaped their attention and learn which features are relevant or irrelevant to a new concept' (Bransford et al. 1999: 48). This book is about how such communities can be created and why teachers are so important in the process of creating these communities.

Drawing on examples from classroom practice Chapter 7 examines different ways in which teachers can design and orchestrate mathematical learning environments. The word 'design' restores agency to the teacher, and brings with it the idea of iteration, redesign and tools for design. The idea of designing for learning draws on work on design experiments,[17] but also creatively transforms these ideas, placing teachers at the centre of the design process, within a supportive network of other teachers and researchers.

Focusing on designing for mathematical learning points to the importance of anticipating the ways in which students will engage with solving mathematical problems in the classroom. This is very different from lesson planning which prescribes in minute detail what a teacher will do in each part of a lesson. Designing for learning scopes a problem from a top-level perspective of 'big mathematical ideas' which then enable a teacher to suspend this pre-planning and behave more contingently in the classroom, acting in the moment as they interact with students. These ideas are discussed more fully in Chapters 7 and 8.

Disjunctions between research, policy and practice

Whereas we now know considerably more about how young people learn mathematics than was the case 50 years ago, we are only just beginning to understand the relationship between teaching and learning mathematics. This is because much of the earlier research on learning mathematics was not linked to research on teaching mathematics. So for example the important work on children's' misconceptions in mathematics[18] did not attempt to link results about learning to practices of teaching. Nonetheless this early research influenced educational reforms in the UK and other countries around the world. For example, research on children's learning of algebra and the difficulties they have with the use of symbols in mathematics[19] led to a rethinking of the algebra curriculum in many countries, a rethinking that was often accompanied by an under-emphasis on the role of symbolic algebra.[20] In England, for example, the argument was made that the advent of computers would reduce the need for algebra and for almost a decade symbolic algebra almost disappeared from the pre-16 curriculum. We now understand more about the ways in which symbolic algebra does still have a role to play in mathematics education, despite the advent of computer-based algebra systems. This relates to the idea of symbol sense[21] and an understanding of the role of symbols as tools for transforming thinking which is discussed more fully in Chapter 6.

Research is often taken up and transformed by policy makers and practitioners. In this process research results become simplified and transformed into 'slogans' such as 'informal methods', 'readiness' and 'scaffolding' which take on a life of their own, separate from the complexity of the teaching and learning theory from which they emanated. It is this over-simplification process which is potentially damaging to classroom practice. In Chapter 10 I argue that teachers have to be more than technicians and 'deliverers' if we want young people to develop flexible and rich mathematical knowledge. In this sense there is a need to break the one-way relationship between research results and classroom practice through critical debate and iterative refining of research results within a community which incorporates both teachers and academics.

Concluding remarks

In many countries around the world each new decade has heralded school reforms which embody new approaches to teaching mathematics. These reforms increasingly draw on research evidence. Yet there appears to have been very little effect of these reforms on students' enhanced pleasure from and learning of mathematics. Why is this the case? Is it because educational change is often driven by a political agenda with no time allowed for learning from previous reforms? Is it because there is little understanding about the processes of transforming educational research into practice? Or is it because educational research has only begun to touch on the complex and dynamic processes of teaching and learning mathematics? I suggest that it is the last question which begins to get to the heart of why educational research has had very little constructive impact on educational practice.

If the processes of questioning and inquiry are what drives the learning of mathematics, it is also questioning and inquiry that drive learning about teaching and learning mathematics. So what is the role of a 'book' in this process? It could be argued that a book is an unproductive way of communicating ideas about teaching and learning mathematics. And indeed a book can only be a starting point in provoking you to ask your own questions and in supporting you to find ways of answering such questions.

I have set myself the challenge of writing a book which brings together ideas about teaching and learning mathematics which have surrounded my own history of teaching and researching mathematics. And in responding to this challenge I have developed new ideas through the very process of writing itself. This, I would argue, is always the case. We do not know before we write, and we do not know before we speak.

Notes

1. See for example Bishop et al. (1996). English (2002).
2. Hatfield Polytechnic, now the University of Hertfordshire.
3. See Hoyles and Sutherland (1989) and Sutherland (1992).
4. For example Papert (1980).
5. For further discussion of the context of this quote, which is taken from the work of the InterActive Education project see Chapter 8.
6. Japanese teachers often work together in a school to collectively study lessons. This is called the Lesson Study Method. For further information see Fernandez (2002).
7. For example behaviourism, constructivism and embodied cognition. For an overview of such theoretical perspectives see Davis et al. (2000).
8. The idea of liberating constraints is taken from Davis et al. (2000).
9. See Vygotsky (1978), Wertsch (1985, 1998), Bruner (1996), Kazulin et al. (2003), Steiner and Mahn (1996).
10. For further discussion of this see Joseph (1992) and Gallardo (2001).
11. For further discussion of the use of the number line in primary schools see for example Beishuizen (1999).
12. These are connected objects which focus on the notion of place value in arithmetic; see Dienes (1960).
13. The abacus is a mechanical aid used for counting.
14. Maple is a tool for solving mathematical problems and creating interactive technical applications; see www.maplesoft.com.
15. Wertsch and Sohmer (1995).
16. See Daniels (2001).
17. For further discussion of this see Kelly (2003).
18. For example Hart et al. (1981).
19. For example Küchemann (1981).
20. For further discussion of this see Royal Society/JMC (1997).
21. See Arcavi (1994, 2005) for further discussion of symbol sense.

2 Cultures of Mathematics Education

Opening remarks

> The communications and expectations of what it means to be a learner of mathematics in the classroom emerge through the interactions of the students with their teacher and each other. Crucial to this process are the students' explorations of what mathematics is and what it means to them to do mathematics so that what emerges is a genuine confluences of the culture of each participant.
>
> (Brown and Coles 2003: 151)

We tend to assume that school mathematics is a culture-free subject – more or less the same around the world. This may be because mathematicians view mathematics as such and through their international communities work hard to construct 'mathematics' in this way. However, within this chapter I shall argue that school mathematics is not culture-free. Approaches to teaching, assessment, curricula, textbooks, tools, knowledge and teacher education all vary from country to country. These differences impact on both the mathematics education culture which is constituted in a particular classroom and the mathematics which students learn in school.

What is meant by culture and more specifically mathematics education culture? As a starting point I take the loose definition of culture developed by colleagues at the University of Bristol.[1] A culture reflects the practices of a group of people who are in communication with each other, and who share, knowingly or not, some common sense of what purposes and activities are important. The group acts as if certain things matter and others do not, and as if some things are 'obvious' or 'natural' and others 'ridiculous' or 'impossible'. In this respect values and purposes are enshrined in the language, symbols, material objects and environments which the group has fashioned. Cultures are dynamic, changing over time, as is very much the case with education cultures.

By focusing on mathematics education culture the aim of this chapter is to draw attention to the constraints and possibilities of the local situation within which a teacher works. My argument is that the more teachers understand these the more they are liberated to act in personally meaningful ways. Here I draw on the ideas of Davis et al. (2000: 88) who suggest that 'teachers can enhance creative activity by placing appropriate constraints on the range of possibilities'.

The chapter starts by highlighting similarities and differences between national curricula, because the curriculum is one of the major structures which influences what a teacher 'can do' in the classroom. It then moves on to compare mathematics textbooks from different countries as these are examples of material objects which have been fashioned by the people within a mathematics education culture. Finally I discuss the emerging literature which compares teaching mathematics in different countries.

Mathematics curricula

Nowadays many countries have a specified National Curriculum for Mathematics, although in the history of education in the UK this is a relatively recent phenomenon.[2] I first became aware of the similarities and differences between national curricula when I was working on a collaborative project with Teresa Rojano, from Mexico. We gradually realized the rather substantial differences in approaches to algebra and functions and graphs in the two countries.[3] These differences were often manifested in the ways in which students solved and explained their solution to a range of problems. For example, when solving a problem which involved interpolating information from a distance time graph Mexican students tended to draw on algorithmic methods (for example the 'rule of three') whereas British students were more likely to estimate the solution. When solving an algebraic equation Mexican students were more likely to manipulate the equation in order to find a solution, whereas British students were more likely to use an informal 'trial-and-refinement' approach.

This awareness evolved as I co-ordinated a working group on algebraic thinking which culminated in the book *Perspectives on School Algebra* (Sutherland et al. 2000).[4]

> Many of the difficulties we encountered when working as a group related to views about what is and what is not algebra. A related issue which soon emerged from the work of the group is that school algebra differs in its emphasis from country to country ... for example in some countries students are likely to engage in carefully crafted word problems which have traditionally been designed to engage students in constructing algebraic methods while in other countries these types of problems have almost disappeared from the curriculum. As we have pointed out before the meanings which students construct for algebra will be related to the types of problems which are prioritised in the classroom.
>
> (Lins et al. 2001: 8)

Schmidt et al. (1997) have documented the extensive differences in the organization and structure of mathematics curricula, for example in terms of how situations are represented mathematically, the role of generalizing and justifying and the extent of the emphasis on performing routine procedures. More recently I carried out a study which compared the algebra curriculum from a range of countries (Sutherland 2002). The study found similarities between the continental European countries (France, Germany, Hungary, Italy) in their emphasis on algebra as a study of systems of equations and inequalities and on their treatment of functions as a separate strand of the curriculum. In contrast the UK, Australia and Canada placed more of an emphasis on algebra as a means of expressing generality and patterns. Whereas the idea of introducing algebra within the context of problem situations was evident within most of the curricula, within some countries these 'problem situations' were sometimes more traditional word problems (for example in Italy, Hungary, France, Hong Kong) and within other countries they were more 'realistic modelling situations' (Canada, Australia, UK). In general where there was more emphasis on solving 'realistic problems' there tended to be less emphasis on symbolic manipulation.

Celia Hoyles and colleagues (2002) carried out a similar study which compared geometry curricula focusing on using and applying geometry (particularly in relation to proof), geometrical reasoning, transformation and coordinates and measures and construction. This study found differences between the nature and extent of geometry within the curriculum. For example, in some countries a more practical or realistic approach to geometry is taken (for example The Netherlands) and in other countries a more theoretical approach is taken (for example Japan, France). The geometry study also found differences with respect to mathematical proof:

> In some countries, given their orientation towards geometry (e.g. The Netherlands), proof is not mentioned at all; in others, students are encouraged to discover and use the results of proofs rather than to construct for themselves (Ontario); another group of countries seem to encourage explanation as a basis for simple proofs. At the other extreme, students are expected to construct formal proofs (e.g. France and Japan and selected students in Baden-Württemberg and Lucerne).
>
> (2002: 3)

These studies illustrate that school mathematics has evolved differently in different countries, and this relates as much to the school systems and approaches to pedagogy as it does to views about mathematics. Whereas what is specified in a mathematics curriculum is only one aspect of the multi-faceted influences on how a mathematics teacher approaches teaching in the classroom, the fact that so many differences emerge in the specification of national curricula does suggest that different mathematics cultures prevail around the world.

Textbooks and mathematics education culture

Mathematics textbooks are used in different ways by teachers, but almost every country produces its own textbooks and these reflect the beliefs and practices of a particular mathematics education culture. A socio-cultural perspective suggests that the meanings which students construct as they engage with a textbook page will be influenced by the ways in which mathematics is structured and presented on the page. In some countries (for example France, Singapore, Japan, Hungary) textbook writers appear to pay attention to the ways in which mathematics is represented on the page (see for example Figure 2.1). In other countries (for example the United States and Britain) textbook writers pay much less attention to the structural aspects of how mathematics is represented. This is illustrated by the image in Figure 2.2 where more attention has been paid to what has been called the 'decorative aspects' of presentation. Possibly these textbook writers believe that these 'decorative aspects' will motivate students to learn mathematics, although it is not clear that this is the case.

This difference in emphasis is illustrated by a comparison of the way in which multiplication is introduced within primary mathematics textbooks in France, the UK, Hungary and Singapore.[5] In France multiplication is first introduced to 7–8-year-olds through the ideas of 'repeated addition' and 'numbers of objects in a rectangular array'. From the beginning the 'x' sign is introduced and the emphasis is on the commutativity of multiplication. The teacher's guide to this sequence of lessons suggests that the 'x' sign is introduced as a valuable way of naming an m by n array (i.e. 3 × 4 is the name for a 3 by 4 array). Later in the textbook for 7–8-year-olds multiplication is introduced as the notion of repeated jumps on a number line, with the idea of commutativity still being emphasized. Standard algorithms for multiplying multidigit numbers begin to be introduced at the end of the year in which students are 8–9. Diagrams are used extensively throughout the texts to help students move from tools which have been introduced for pedagogic purposes (for example m by n array of squares) and standard algorithms for multiplication (see Figure 2.3).

In a Singapore textbook the idea of multiplication is first introduced when students are aged 6–7 as 'repeated addition of equal groups' (see Figure 2.1).

The accompanying teacher's guide draws attention to the part-whole approach for introducing multiplication, which has already been used for

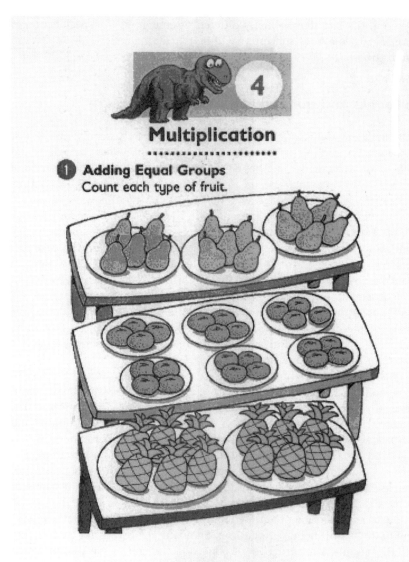

Figure 2.1 Multiplication excerpt from Singapore primary mathematics textbook

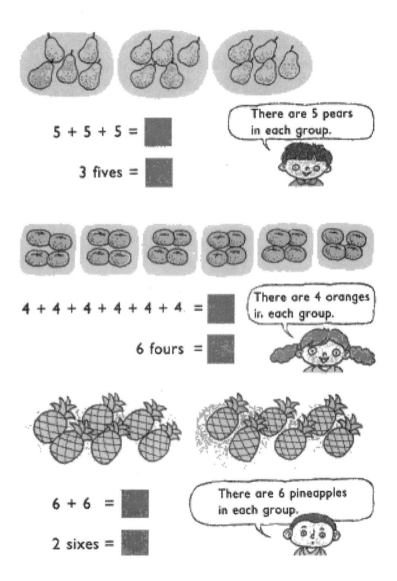

$5 + 5 + 5 =$ ▮

There are 5 pears in each group.

3 fives $=$ ▮

$4 + 4 + 4 + 4 + 4 + 4 =$ ▮

There are 4 oranges in each group.

6 fours $=$ ▮

$6 + 6 =$ ▮

There are 6 pineapples in each group.

2 sixes $=$ ▮

■ Best ways ■ ■ ■ ■ ■ ■

There are many different ways
to work out difficult multiplications.

```
        34 x 27              34                34
       ↙     ↘             x  27             x  27
    34         34          238  (34 x 7)      340  (34 x 10)
   x 20       x  7        + 680  (34 x 20)    340  (34 x 10)
   ─────      ─────        ─────             + 238  (34 x 7)
    680        238          918               ─────
       ↘      ↙              1                 918
        680                                     1
       + 238
       ─────
        918
```

1 Decide the best way to find the products
   of these. Show all your workings-out. .

   a 45 x 35   b 31 x 12   c 16 x 45
   d 57 x 21   e 72 x 26   f 69 x 18

2 Check each product in [1] by multiplying
   in reverse order. For example, for a you will
   calculate 35 x 45.

3 Decide the best way to solve these problems.

   a A day trip by coach to Blackpool costs £27
     for adults and £16 for children.
     If 30 adults and 13 children go, what will be
     the total cost of fares?

   b Sarah works a 38-hour week at a Blackpool hotel
     and has 6 weeks holiday each year.
     How many hours does she work
     in a complete year?

   c A stick of rock is 28 cm long.
     What length of rock would be needed
     to make a box of 48 sticks?

4 If 25 is the 5th square number,
   what is the 42nd square number?

   Now try page 31.

30

STEPS 5:7

Figure 2.2 Excerpt from English primary mathematics textbook

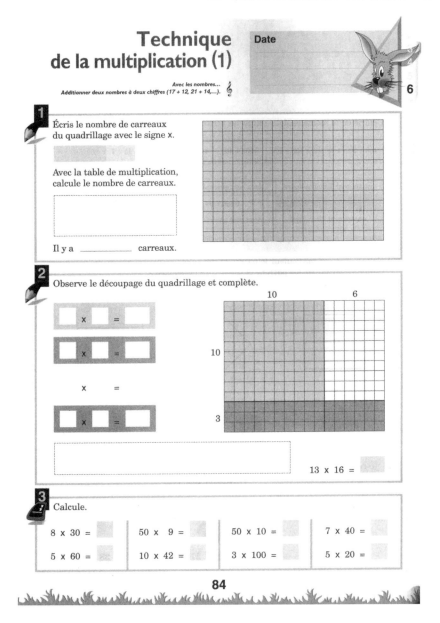

Figure 2.3 Multiplication – excerpt from French primary mathematics textbook

Unit 4: Multiplication

① Adding Equal Groups

Textbook 1B Pages 42 to 45
Workbook Exercises 30 to 32

Instructional Objectives

- To recognise equal groups and find the total number in the groups by repeated addition.
- To use the mathematical language such as '4 threes' and '2 groups of 5' to describe equal groups.

Notes for Teachers

When a whole is made up of two parts,

- we *add* to find the whole given the two parts;
- we *subtract* to find one part given the whole and the other part.

For example,

$4 + 3 = 7, \ 3 + 4 = 7$
$7 - 3 = 4, \ 7 - 4 = 3$

The part-whole concept of addition and subtraction can be extended to multiplication and division.

When a whole is made up of equal parts,

- we *multiply* to find the whole given the number of parts and the number in each part;
- we *divide* to find the number in each part given the whole and the number of parts; or
- we *divide* to find the number of parts given the whole and the number in each part.

For example,

$4 \times 3 = 12, \ 3 \times 4 = 12$
$12 \div 3 = 4, \ 12 \div 4 = 3$

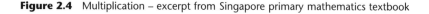

Figure 2.4 Multiplication – excerpt from Singapore primary mathematics textbook

addition and subtraction (see Figure 2.4). Throughout the Singaporean text attention seems to be paid to the linking of a diagrammatic representation to a symbolic representation (see Figure 2.1). The 'x' sign is introduced as 'This is multiplication. It means putting together equal groups'. In the teacher's guide it says, 'The students develop and use the language of multiplication through telling number stories such as: There are 4 vases. There are 5 flowers in each vase. There are 20 flowers altogether. 4 × 5 = 20'.

This emphasis on linking multiple representations is also evident in the Hungarian text (Figure 2.5). As in the French and Singaporean texts different ways of representing multiplication are all linked together, with pictures, words and symbolic representations appearing together on the textbook page.

In contrast to these three countries the British textbook studied appears to be more haphazard in its use of mathematical representations when introducing students to multiplication. When multiplication is first introduced images of equal groups are presented together with a symbolic representation of 4 + 4 + 4 = ... Students are not introduced to the multiplication

Szorzás

Peti 3 doboz bonbont vett. Minden dobozban 5 bonbon volt.
Hány bonbont vett összesen?

$5 + 5 + 5 =$ 1 5 ⎫
3-szor 5 = 1 5 ⎭

Röviden így írhatjuk:

$3 \cdot 5 = 1\ 5$

Réka 5 doboz bonbont vett. Minden dobozban 3 bonbon volt.
Hány bonbont vett összesen?

$3 + 3 + 3 + 3 + 3 =$ 1 5 ⎫
5-ször 3 = 1 5 ⎭

Röviden így írhatjuk:

$5 \cdot 3 = 1\ 5$

A szorzásban a **tényezők** felcserélhetők: $3 \cdot 5 = 5 \cdot 3$
Ezért ezt: $3 \cdot 5$, így olvashatjuk: **3-szor 5,**

3 szorozva 5-tel,

a 3-nak 5-szöröse stb.

Figure 2.5 Multiplication – excerpt from Hungarian primary mathematics textbook

symbol (x) at this stage. This separation of a standard mathematical symbol from a mathematical concept appears to be a characteristic of British primary mathematics textbooks, whereas the French, Singaporean and Hungarian texts analysed all introduce standard mathematical symbols at the same time as a concept is being introduced. When the x symbol is introduced for the first time in the British textbook (Figure 2.6) the emphasis seems to be on pictorial representations which 'might' motivate students to engage with the task and not on the relationship between the symbolic representation of multi-plication and the diagrammatic representation of multiplication. So for example in the 'help box' in Figure 2.6 students are more likely to pay attention to the pictorial images on the 'set of stickers' than on the rela-tionship between the symbolic notation 4 × 2 and the 4 × 2 array of stickers.

Superficial analysis of these primary textbooks could suggest that mathematics is treated in a similar way in all four countries, all students are introduced to multiplication as repeated addition, multiplication as jumps on a number line and multiplication as a way of representing a two-dimensional array. It is only by paying attention to the detail of the presented images that different views about what mathematics is, how students learn mathematics and how mathematics should be taught emerge. Presentations in textbooks from Hungary, France and Singapore structure the page so that students are

Split and multiply ▪ ▪ ▪ ▪ [straw]

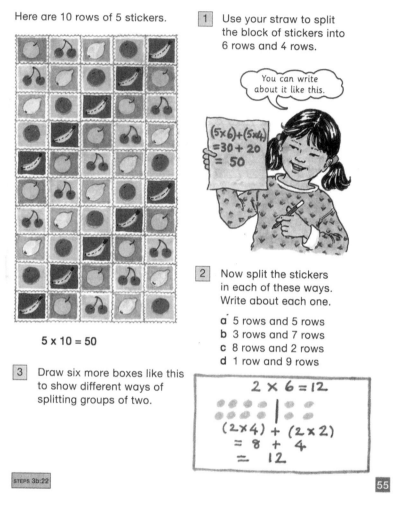

Here are 10 rows of 5 stickers.

1 Use your straw to split the block of stickers into 6 rows and 4 rows.

You can write about it like this.

$(5 \times 6) + (5 \times 4)$
$= 30 + 20$
$= 50$

$5 \times 10 = 50$

2 Now split the stickers in each of these ways. Write about each one.

a 5 rows and 5 rows
b 3 rows and 7 rows
c 8 rows and 2 rows
d 1 row and 9 rows

3 Draw six more boxes like this to show different ways of splitting groups of two.

$2 \times 6 = 12$

$(2 \times 4) + (2 \times 2)$
$= 8 + 4$
$= 12$

[STEPS 3b:22]   [55]

Figure 2.6 Multiplication – excerpt from English primary mathematics textbook

more likely to read the link between the symbolic notation for multiplication and the m × n array (see for example Figures 2.3, 2.4, 2.5). Here mathematical symbolic notation is almost always closely linked to images which support the structure of the notation. In contrast the UK teacher's guide implicitly suggests that students should first understand an idea and that after this understanding the mathematical notation can be introduced. Also whereas the teacher's guides in the Singapore and French schemes set out to explain the purpose behind the way in which mathematics is represented to students, the teacher's guide which accompanies the British scheme is much more illusive in this respect. The idea that it is important to understand an idea before representing it symbolically is liked to an implicit Piagetian theory of learning in which the emphasis is on understanding before symbolizing.[6] In contrast a Vygotskian and socio-cultural approach emphasizes the role of symbols as being inextricably linked to the process of understanding.

Reflecting on this comparative study of primary mathematics textbooks after a number of years it appears even clearer to me that the authors of the British textbook scheme did not believe that the mathematics we learn relates to the ways in which it is represented on a page. This lack of attention to the role of external representations and symbols in the process of coming to understand a mathematical idea in primary mathematics is similar to the lack of emphasis on or even avoidance of algebraic symbols which was evident in secondary mathematics at this time.[7]

Research by Birgit Pepin and Linda Haggarty (2002: 22) also identified substantial differences in the way in which mathematics is represented in secondary mathematics textbooks. Focusing mainly on the connections which are made between mathematical topics, they report that 'Whereas in some countries students are inundated with skills, procedures and dis-connected mathematical knowledge, in others students are allowed to develop an appreciation of its interconnectedness and generalisable nature'.[8]

In summary there are huge differences between the ways in which mathematics is represented in textbooks in different countries. These differences relate to different beliefs about learning mathematics and different beliefs about the role of language and symbols in mathematics. These differences are likely to be reflected in practices of teaching in the classroom, which will in turn relate to differences in learning mathematics.

Approaches to teaching mathematics

There is increasing evidence from video studies of classrooms around the world that the ways in which mathematics is taught in schools is approached differently in different countries. The work of the TIMSS[9] video study carried out by Stigler and colleagues was one of the first studies to draw attention to similarities and differences between countries The first video study compared 8th-grade classes in Germany, Japan and the USA (Stigler and Hiebert 1997) and reported that German and Japanese teachers place more emphasis on developing concepts than did teachers from the USA. Moreover 'Japanese students spent less time practising routine procedures and more time inventing, analysing and proving than their peers in the other countries' (1997: 17).

Interestingly these studies have convincingly shown that the countries with high levels of achievement on TIMSS do not all use teaching approaches with similar characteristics. In particular both Hong Kong and Japanese students perform highly in international comparative mathematics tests but mathematics lessons in these countries appear to have different characteristics. For example, Japanse lessons are characterized by students being asked to make mathematical connections, whereas Hong Kong lessons are characterized by students being asked to follow mathematical procedures.

More recently David Clarke and colleagues in their Learners' Perspectives Study are identifying the interrelationship between students' and teachers' practices in mathematics classrooms and comparing similarities and differences between countries.[10] They are identifying structural differences in mathematics classroom practices even between countries as superficially similar in culture as Australia and the USA.[11] This work is highlighting the problem of polarizing teaching and learning into either teacher-led or student-centred positions:

> Teacher-dominating classrooms in Confucian-heritage cultures are always seen as an environment not conducive to learning in western countries. However, recent studies have shown that students learning in such classrooms can still give very good performances. Therefore it seems that simple labels of 'teacher-dominating' or 'student-centred' have not explained the crux of the matter.
>
> (Mok 2003: 1)

Importantly international comparative studies suggest that analysis of classroom data is not culture-free and that, for example, western analyses of Confucian-heritage cultures may bring their own cultural bias to what is important in teaching and learning.[12] This suggests that new methodological approaches need to be developed when comparing teaching and learning mathematics in different countries.

Concluding remarks

In beginning to unpack the similarities and differences between mathematics classrooms around the world it is becoming clear that there is still a considerable amount to be understood about the complexity of teaching and learning mathematics, how the culture of a mathematics classroom is constituted and how countries differ quite considerably in their values, practices and in their common sense of what purposes and activities are important. The TIMSS video study has taken a rather reductionist view of characterizing similarities and differences with considerable emphasis being placed on quantification of certain phenomena. This does not begin to get to the heart of what constitutes a mathematics culture.

David Clarke (2002) quite rightly challenges the simplistic identification of culture with nationality, pointing out that the culture of the classroom can be constructed differently within a particular country or school system. However, he argues that comparative studies can be used as a mirror to help us understand more about ourselves, more about our own systems and the constraints within which we are working.

Teachers have to teach within the constraints of their own local systems. They cannot transcend their own local culture. However, an awareness and unpacking of the constraints and possibilities of a local situation can help in making decisions about how to teach. In this respect national and regional strategies can be reconceptualized as mediating tools that could constrain or enhance a teacher's way of working. Whatever the structuring constraints I agree with Brousseau (1997) that 'learning mathematics' has to be the stake of what is at issue in the classroom, not 'guess what is in the teacher's head' or 'how can I pass through the hoops of the assessment system'. Taking this as the starting point other resources such as the teacher's knowledge and the assessment system can be harnessed in a productive way for this overall purpose.

Notes

1. For further discussion of this see Sutherland et al. (2003).
2. A national curriculum was first introduced in England and Wales in 1989. To get a sense of some of the debate which surrounded its introduction see Dowling and Noss (1990) and Brown (1996).
3. See for example Rojano et al. (1996) and Molyneux-Hodgson et al. (2000).
4. This derived from a working group of the International Group for the Psychology of Mathematics Education.
5. For a more extensive discussion of this work see Harries and Sutherland (1999).
6. For further discussion of this see Sutherland (1993a).
7. For further discussion of this see Chapter 6.
8. Pepin and Haggarty compared secondary mathematics textbooks from the UK France and Germany.
9. Trends in International Mathematics and Science Study (TIMSS, formerly known as the Third International Mathematics and Science Study); see http://timss.bc.edu/. Also see Schmidt et al. (1997).
10. For more information on the the Learners' Perspectives' Study see http://extranet.edfac.unimelb.edu.au/DSME/lps/
11. See Mesiti and Clarke (2003).
12. For further discussion of this see Leung (1995, 2005) and Mok (2003).

3 Ways of Knowing Mathematics

Now to pedagogy. Early on, children encounter the hoary distinction between what is known by 'us' (friends, parents, teachers, and so on) and what in some larger sense is simply 'known'. In these post-positivist, perhaps 'post-modern' times, we recognise all too well that the 'known' is neither God-given truth nor, as it were, written irrevocably in the Book of nature. Knowledge in this dispensation is always putatively revisable. But revisability is not to be confused with free-for-all relativism, the view that since no theory is the ultimate truth, all theories, like all people, are equal. We surely recognise the distinction between Popper's 'World-Two' of personally held beliefs, hunches, and opinions and his 'World Three' of justified knowledge. But what makes the latter 'objective' is not that it constitutes some positivist's free-standing, aboriginal reality, but rather that it has stood up to sustained scrutiny and been tested by the best available evidence.

(Bruner 1996: 61)

Diversity and learning

As humans we are constantly trying to make sense of our world, we are irrepressible theorizers. This making sense leads us to construct our own personal theories, our own personal knowledge. Consider the following extract of a conversation with Eloise, a 15-year-old student. Eloise at age 15 was in the bottom set of students in her year group.[1] When interviewed about the meaning she gave to the use of letters in mathematics she told the interviewer that the value of a letter related to its position in the alphabet. When probed further she provided the following explanation:

Int: Does L have to be a larger number than A?
Eloise: Yes because A starts off as 1 or something.
Int: What made you think that [L has to be a larger number than A]?
Eloise: Because when we were little we used to do a code like that ... in junior school ... A would equal 1, B equals 2, C equals 3 ... were possibilities of A being 5 and B being 10 and that lot ... but it would come up too high a number to do it ... it was always in some order...

Eloise had developed her own theory about the meaning of letters which derived from her work in primary school, and made sense in the context of the problems she was solving at the time. This personal knowledge had not been intentially taught by the teacher and was no longer appropriate (or correct) in the context of secondary-school mathematics. Eloise's theory about letters would have influenced how she made sense of letters when she encountered them in secondary-school mathematics. This is why the teacher has an important role in that 'appropriately arranged contrasts can help people notice new features that previously escaped their attention and learn which features are relevant or irrelevant to a new concept' (Bransford et al. 1999: 48). Eloise did in fact begin to shift her interpretation of letters through work with spreadsheets and how this happened is discussed more fully in Chapter 6.

What this example illustrates is that each student brings to the classroom their own history of learning and, when faced with a new situation, makes sense of this from their own particular experience and way of knowing. There are different approaches to interpreting Eloise's personal knowing which was constructed by Eloise. One approach is to consider her knowing as a 'misconception', a temporary pathology to be eradicated by appropriate teaching. This approach is problematic because it does not take into account the fact that so called 'misconceptions' are actually conceptions which work in particular situations.[2] As Brousseau (1997: 82) has pointed out:

> Errors and failures do not have the simplified role that we would like them to play. Errors are not only the effect of ignorance, of uncertainty, of chance, espoused by empiricists or behaviourist learning theories, but the effect of a previous piece of knowledge which was interesting and successful, but which now is revealed as false or simply unadapted . . . the error is a component of the meaning of the acquired piece of knowledge.

Out-of-school mathematical practices

Students not only bring their previous school experiences of mathematics to a new learning situation, but they also bring their experiences from out of school. Throughout their school years young people participate with adults and other young people in a whole range of everyday leisure and work-related mathematical practices which could impact on school mathematics, for example playing card games, helping with DIY around the home, planning a holiday, working in a shop or working alongside an older sibling as they carry out their homework.

Moll and Greenberg (1992: 320) suggest that households are in fact educational settings in which the main function is to 'transmit knowledge that enhances the survival of its dependents'. Their work with Mexican families has drawn attention to the functioning of dense social networks which 'facilitate different forms of economic assistance and labour cooperation that help families avoid the expenses involved in using secondary institutions, such as plumbing companies or automobile repair shops' (p. 321). They call the social sharing of knowledge between families the exchange of 'funds of knowledge'. They provide an example of Juan (6th grade) who has a bicycle shop in the back of his house, in which he swops used parts, and assembles parts into bicycles, which he then sells. Juan's sisters, Carmen and Zoraida, sell candy which their mother buys in Nogales (a border town in Mexico). Moll and Greenberg emphasize that most young people learn through participation in whatever is the economic activity of the household. They point out that 'it is very easy for outsiders (educators) to underestimate the wealth of funds of knowledge available in working-class households. Funds of knowledge are available in these households regardless of the families' years of formal schooling of prominence assigned to literacy' (p. 327).

Recent work by Martin Hughes and colleagues has also documented a whole range of out-of-school practices which are likely to impact on learning mathematics in school, from playing games, to checking shopping bills. They discuss the case of Nadia, from a Bangladeshi family in Cardiff:

> Nadia described extensive use of mathematics in her out-of-school life. For example, she always accompanies her mother to the shops because she is needed to check the shopping list, read labels, and check the goods against the receipt. Nadia's mother is sometimes confused about numerals because of the similarity of different numbers in Bengali and Western scripts: she points out, for example, that the Bengali for '4' looks like an '8' to the Western eye. Nadia's role is therefore to help her mother check the receipts to avoid being 'cheated'. Nadia gives her father a 'bill' each week for her pocket money, and he will often test her by giving part of the money and asking her how much more she needs. Nadia also records her pocket money in a notebook, so that she knows how much her father owes her.
>
> (Winter et al. 2004: 68)

Nadia explained to the researchers how she uses a whole range of tools for supporting her mathematical work at home. She uses a calculator at home to check her homework and other mathematical calculations. She also uses a whiteboard, which is on her bedroom wall, to carry out calculations.

The work of Baker et al. (2003) also highlights the myriad ways in which primary-school pupils develop numeracy practices at home. They discuss how Aaysha, a 5-year-old from a Pakistani family, was able to use both a finger-counting-in-threes method she had learned at home and a finger-counting-in-ones method taught at school. Aaysha appeared to use three-to-a-finger methods for bigger number problems, and in this sense was learning for herself which was the most useful tool for which type of problem. We also know from research on street mathematics (Nunes et al. 1993) that young people learn very effective 'mathematical' strategies for solving 'street problems' without ever having attended school. More importantly, we know that young people can be successful with street mathematics and yet fail in school.

What these studies suggest is that all young people are likely to be engaging in mathematically related practices out of school, which impact on what they learn in school. They also highlight the ways in which young people are resourceful learners out of school, an issue which I shall return to later in this chapter.

Mathematics and out-of-school uses of ICT

Nowadays in many countries around the world the vast majority of young people have access to computers out of school[3] and the computer provides a range of new mathematically related ICT (information and communication technology) tools. Consider the following conversation with two 8-year-olds from a primary school in Bristol:[4]

Int: Do either of you use Excel at home [Alan shakes head]?
Ray: Sometimes. My Dad uses it for his paperwork.
Int: And when you use it what do you use it for?
Ray: Umm, he uses it, cos when he's got paper calculations and some are hard, like, for him, he puts it in Excel and then he puts, he circles it and then presses the equal button and it tells him what the sums are.
Int: What do you use it for?
Ray: Maths homework.
Alan: Cheat.

From sitting alongside his father at home Ray had observed him using a spreadsheet for his work. Ray's explanation shows that he understands how a spreadsheet can carry out 'hard' calculations. Interestingly, until this interview was carried out by a researcher the class teacher was not aware of this 'fund of knowledge', illustrating the way in which home learning is often not recognized at school.

Another example is the case of Alistair, a primary-school pupil.[5] Alistair chose computer programming as an out-of-school leisure activity, although he had first been introduced to Basic programming in an after-school club at primary school. At home he started to use Basic programming to solve problems which he realized would be difficult with paper-and-pencil mathematics:

Alistair: And there are some things in programming which you just can't work out with maths, well I've found you can't work out. There aren't procedures that have already been defined to do that, like find a prime number. That would detect if something's a prime number. Then I have to develop my own method of working that out.

Int: And what method did you choose in the end?

Alistair: I made the procedure up myself. It was something like, start with one number, well is it a prime number, you first divide the number by half the number and then round that down to whatever the number is without any decimal places. And then times it by 2 again because you halved the number. If it's the same as the number you want to find if it's a prime then do something or other, I've forgotten ... First, divide it by 2, round it down to no decimal places and then ...

Int: So that would be 3.5 and then 3.

Alistair: And then it would times it by 2 again and see if it was the same answer. If it is then it's not a prime number. And then it divides it by 3 and then rounds it down and then times it by 3 and does it all the way up to value of the number. Like, say if it was 7 it would do all the way up to dividing it by 6 because ...

Int: Oh so it's testing if something divides into it. Okay, so you're testing to see whether all those numbers go into it are you?

Alistair: Yeah.

Int: That seems very intriguing, very clever.

Alistair: Excluding the number itself and 1 because they do divide by themselves.

These explanations point to Alistair's awareness and understanding of prime numbers, an understanding which is likely to have evolved through the process of constructing computer programmes. Alistair had discovered the powerful potential of computer programming, a potential which, as I discuss further in Chapter 6, draws on the culture of mathematics. The case of Alistair showed how through computer programming at home he bumped into a whole range of mathematical ideas, such as Cartesian coordinates, the difference between integers and decimals, properties of circles and the idea of variable. This learning of mathematical ideas at home also overlapped with what he needed to learn at school (at age 10) although, as he explained to us, it was his father's girlfriend who helped him make the links between mathematics for programming and mathematics for school:

Alistair:	I'm the only one that did the test.[6]
Int:	And what sort of things were there?
Alistair:	Um, find the area of the second square if the area of the first square is something or other, something or other, and find the perimeter of these ... I think it was two semi circles in line and they say find the perimeter, yes. Perimeter? Is that the right word? Yes, perimeter. Um that sort of thing and algebra.
Int:	What sort of algebra's that?
Alistair:	Um, mainly equations and that sort of thing.
Int:	For example?
Alistair:	Y5 = Y3 + 10, something like that.
Int:	Y5, why's it called Y5.
Alistair:	5 times Y.
Int:	5Y. Has your teacher told you all this?
Alistair:	Uh ... no.
Int:	How come you can do it then?
Alistair:	My dad's girlfriend told me about it.
Int:	Told you about algebra?
Alistair:	Yeah.
Int:	Why ... is she a maths teacher or something?
Alistair:	No, she just sort of happens to know some things about maths that I need to know for my Level 6. I mean it's not like a really hard test, you just need basic knowledge of how to find the area of things and that sort of thing.

This example illustrates the type of home–school knowledge-exchange which occurred as Alistair moved between the world of home and the world of school. Alistair's primary-school teacher did not appear to be aware of what mathematics Alistair was learning through computer programming at home, and was more interested in why he did not use a word processor to do his homework:

> But really I don't know what he was using at home and he rarely came to school with work done on a computer, which is quite interesting because his handwriting is appalling. And I really encourage children to use the computers at home for homework. I don't know why he didn't. The only thing I can think of was, you know, that was completely schoolwork and this is home.

Interestingly, Alistair's learning of programming reached a ceiling when he challenged himself to learn how to program in Visual Basic:

Alistair: My problem is I haven't got, like, anyone to give me any ideas of actually what to do really.

He realized that he needed to work with someone who knew about Visual Basic and appreciated the conceptual gap between Visual Basic and the Basic language he had already taught himself:

Alistair: You jump across to Visual Basic and there's this giant gaping black void beneath you.

This suggests that whereas informal and independent learning strategies are adequate for learning about some knowledge domains there are other domains where it is almost impossible for a 'lone student' to learn such knowledge without the support of 'more knowledgeable others'. This seems to relate to the complexity of the conceptual domain and the zone of proximal development of the student. This issue will be discussed further in Chapter 9.

Scientific and spontaneous concepts

Learning mathematics is about learning to use new tools which enable us to solve problems that would be difficult or impossible to solve with our old tools. For example algebra is a new tool which allows us to solve problems which are very difficult to solve with arithmetic. Unfortunately the long-term benefits of learning to use new mathematical tools cannot always be appreciated in the short term. Paradoxically an emphasis on valuing students' informal approaches could make it even less likely that students see the need for learning a new mathematical tool. This raises the question of how best to introduce new mathematical tools in such a way that students shift from use of old mathematical tools to use of new mathematical tools.

Consider the following example which derives from an interview with a 17-year-old student.[7] Biral explained the approach he used to find the value of t (time) when x (distance) = 80 in the following equation $x = 10 + 20t$:

Biral: I think I used trial and error for that ... say if I did like the t is for seconds and so say if I probably started with about 5 seconds ... 20 times 5 is 100 plus 10 ... that's 110 so that's too much. Then I went down to 4 seconds which is 80, which is 90 ... altogether ... then tried 3.5 seconds...

Int:	Has someone taught you to use that method or did you just work it out yourself?
Biral:	That method I've always, like, used ... just bring it up and down ... but in maths we have been taught to do trial and error ... Such as, when you have to find out ... for instance when you're finding an unknown and you know it's between 2 and 3 and you just use different numbers in between 2 and 3 and then put them back into the formula.

Biral used his calculator to enable him to carry out this 'trial-and-refinement' approach.

As this example illustrates informal 'trial-and-refinement' approaches became taught approaches in British schools. This related to a view that 'any approach' which enables students to solve a problem is better than 'no approach'. For a period in the UK 'trial-and-refinement' methods for solving equations were assessed (see for example Figure 3.1) and used by many students to solve equations (see for example Figure 3.2).

---

17   The equation $x^2 - x - 1 = 0$ has a solution between 1 and 2.
       Use trial and improvement to find this solution correct to 2 decimal places.

       You must show all your trials.

Figure 3.1   Trial and refinement – GCSE examination question

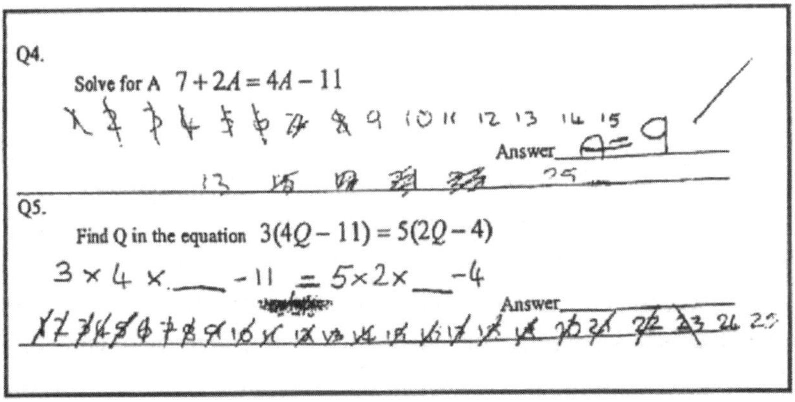

Figure 3.2   Trial and refinement – secondary school pupil methods
Source: Vile 1996.

We can also see evidence of 'any approach' being valued in primary pupils' use of repeated addition for solving 'multiplication problems'

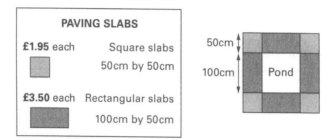

11 Mr Singh buys paving slabs to go around his pond.

PAVING SLABS	
£1.95 each	Square slabs
	50cm by 50cm
£3.50 each	Rectangular slabs
	100cm by 50cm

He buys 4 rectangular slabs and 4 square slabs.

What is the total cost of the slabs he buys?

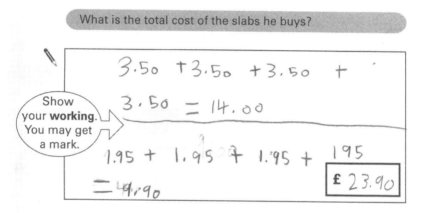

Show your **working**. You may get a mark.

$$3.50 + 3.50 + 3.50 +$$
$$3.50 = 14.00$$

$$1.95 + 1.95 + 1.95 + 195$$
$$= 49.90$$

£ 23.90

Figure 3.3 Repeated addition to solve a primary school Key Stage 2 assessment item

(Figure 3.3). Here the student has used 'repeated addition' to solve a problem which was intended to assess multiplication. This raises the question of whether or not 'any approach' to solving a problem is what should be valued if the overall intention is to teach students to know how to multiply.

So how can students be made aware of new mathematical tools to the extent that they can appreciate that they offer new problem-solving potential? Most adults would agree that multiplication is a powerful and valuable tool, but how can primary pupils become aware of this potential?

It is widely believed by many mathematics teachers and educators that it is possible for students to shift seamlessly from the 'old' to the 'new' mathematical tool, from repeated addition to multiplication, from trial-and-refinement to algebraic equations, from experiment to proof. However, all the evidence suggests that without some sort of direct intervention from a teacher or more knowledgeable other, students do not actually shift their perspective. In Chapter 8 I discuss the way in which Marnie Weeden worked with students so that they shifted their attention from using an experimental approach to learning about mathematical proof. In Chapter 5 I discuss the ways in which Alf Coles engaged students so that they became aware of the potential of using algebraic symbolism. In both of these examples the teacher is facing students with new mathematical tools, enabling them to develop awareness through *use* of the new mathematical tool.

Nicolas Balacheff and I wrote:

> Knowing and knowledge are two faces of the same coin. What we know from the history of mathematical ideas provides evidence for the complexity of the construction of mathematical concepts which places their spontaneous re-discovery out of the reach of the majority of human beings within a reasonable period of time. Schools and teaching are social tools for solving this problem.
>
> (Balacheff and Sutherland 1994: 3)

What we were alluding to here is similar to what Bruner talks about in the quote at the beginning of this chapter: 'what is known by "us" (friends, parents, teachers, and so on) and what in some larger sense is simply "known"'.

Vygotsky (1978) distinguished between spontaneous and scientific concepts. He considered that spontaneous or empirical concepts are developed when children abstract properties from concrete experiences or instances outside the context of explicit instruction. He argued that scientific concepts develop from formal experiences with properties themselves. This 'big picture' approach focuses students' attention on the new conceptual domain and then draws in the old tools/knowledge into this 'big picture'. As Steiner and Mahn (1996: 365) have pointed out Vygotsky recognized the interdependence of everyday and scientific concepts, a dialectic relationship. He believed that everyday concepts feed into the learning of scientific concepts and that

> the dividing line between these two types of concepts turns out to be highly fluid, passing from one side to the other in an infinite number of times in the actual course of development. Right from the start it should be mentioned that the development of spontaneous and academic concepts turn out as processes [sic] which are tightly bound up with one another and which constantly influence one another.

The idea of 'scientific concepts' draws attention to the importance of a systematic organized body of knowledge, the kind of knowledge that can be separated from the community that produced it. Drawing on the work of Popper and Bennet (1992) Bereiter (2002) calls this type of knowledge 'conceptual artefacts'. In this respect he is distinguishing between the physical world (world 1), the subjective or mental world (world 2) and the world of ideas (world 3). He emphasizes that world 3 is not a realm of ultimate truths, it is a human construction. This idea will be taken up again in Chapter 9.

Vygotsky's distinction between scientific and spontaneous concepts also raises the question of the purpose of schooling. One purpose of schooling has to be to enable students to learn knowledge which they would otherwise be unlikely to learn out of school in an empirical inductive way. This suggests that almost all of the mathematics that is part of the curriculum will have to be learned within some sort of school system.

Concluding remarks

This chapter started by focusing on the ways in which young people struggle to find problem-solving approaches and associated explanations when faced with mathematical problems. This becomes their history of mathematical learning which they inevitably bring to any new learning situation. In this sense they develop a range of problem-solving approaches, some of which will be more powerful then others within a particular situation. If they know about addition they will almost spontaneously develop a repeated addition approach to a 'multiplication' problem. They will naturally develop a trial-and-refinement approach to solving an 'algebra problem'. They can develop such approaches without support from a teacher. But without a teacher they will not learn about the powerful new mathematical tool of multiplication or the powerful new mathematical tool of algebra. This leads us back to Bruner's quote at the beginning of the chapter. If we want young people to develop a repertoire of mathematical tools so that they can have the choice to use whatever is the most efficacious for a particular problem-solving situation then they will somehow have to be taught about these new tools.

Notes

1. This example derived from an ESRC-funded project 'The Gap between Arithmetical and Algebraic Thinking' (Sutherland 1993a).
2. The idea of misconceptions and views of knowledge is taken up again in Chapter 9.
3. See for example Facer et al. (2003) and Kent and Facer (2004).
4. Taken from an interview with 8–10-year-old primary-school students, Inter-Active Education Project (Sutherland et al. 2006)

5. Taken from an interview carried out with a 10-year-old boy in the ESRC-funded ScreenPlay Project (Facer et al. 2003).
6. This refers to the Key Stage 2 Standard Assessment Tasks for the end of primary school (age 10–11).
7. Taken from an interview with an A-Level student as part of the project 'The Role of Spreadsheets within School-based Mathematical Practices' (directed by Sutherland and Rojano and funded by the Spencer Foundation).

4 Ways into the World of Mathematics

> When the teacher specifies the practice to be learned, children improvise on the production of that practice but not the practice itself. And it is not possible to resolve problems that are not, in some sense, their own. The more the teacher, the curriculum, the texts, and the lessons, 'own' the problems or decompose steps so as to push learners away from owning problems, the harder it may be for them to develop the practice.
>
> (Lave 1988: 33)

Opening remarks

Mathematical knowledge has developed over centuries, invented and used by people to solve particular problems. We can think of mathematical knowledge as a set of resources or tools and the purpose of mathematics education as being to provide students with access to a wide range of mathematical tools. Linked to such access would be awareness that some mathematical tools are more effective than others, within a particular problem-solving context.

Our choice of mathematical tools relates to the tools we have available, the tools we are knowledgeable about and the particular culture in which we are situated. So, for example, I am very unlikely to use a mathematical tool such as ratio and proportion in the kitchen unless I am working with a recipe which requires precision when scaling up or scaling down. As Hoyles et al. (2001) have shown expert paediactric nurses do not tend to use their taught ratio and proportion methods when calculating drug doses. Instead their calculations on the ward are structured by familiar material units, such as typical dosages for specific drugs and packaging conventions. What these and other similar studies show is that people intelligently use whatever resources they have at hand and that this situated action is structured by cultural practices. Carpenters and builders often solve 'measurement' problems by writing in pencil on an unfinished plastered wall, to compute a long multiplication or even a long division problem. This practice clearly relates to what is for them an efficient and effective way of solving problems on a building site, when paper or a calculator are not readily at hand, and when the problems are too complex to calculate mentally. Here wall and pencil are used as the media for both sketching the objects being measured and calculating a solution. These workings are ephemeral and will eventually be painted over as is the back-of-an-envelope calculation of an engineer. In other situations it is important to keep a record of the problem-solving process, as is often the case in the work of accountants and architects. In other situations mental computation might be the most effective approach, for example when negotiating an on-the-spot business deal.

Paper-based algorithms can also be valuable in certain situations. If I want to carry out the computation 394 × 47 I could possibly manipulate the numbers in my head, using such notions as 47 is 3 less than 50, but I know that I personally cannot rely on purely mental approaches except within simple multiplication problems. If I set out the problem as:

$$394$$
$$47 \times$$

and follow the algorithmic approach, there is a built-in system for me to follow. The way of setting out on paper and the rules which need to be followed support me to produce a correct answer, and the algorithm has been 'designed' for this purpose.

The idea that for any problem situation some mathematical tools are more appropriate than others is not usually acknowledged or discussed in school mathematics. Instead there is a tendency to prioritize a particular approach, for example mental mathematics as opposed to paper and pencil, or paper and pencil as opposed to a calculator. But as I argued in Chapter 2 it is important for students to develop a repertoire of different mathematical tools and an awareness of appropriate use in different situations. This issue will be taken up again in Chapter 9.

Teacher-proofing the classroom?

The traditional view of teaching is that students learn whatever the teacher teaches within a straightforward transmission of knowledge. International research on students' conceptions of mathematics carried out in the early 1980s[1] was truly ground-breaking in that it highlighted the fact that what students learn is not what teachers teach or intend to teach, as the example of Eloise at the beginning of Chapter 3 illustrates. Some of the earlier reactions to the realization that direct teaching does not work resulted in an attempt to teacher-proof the classroom. This led to a proliferation of individualized textbook schemes in England, in an almost direct attempt to by-pass the teacher.[2]

In France there was a similar attempt to by-pass the teacher, with the development of what are called a-didactical situations:

> These are situations in which the mathematics to be learned will appear as the optimal and discoverable solution to the problems posed. The teacher must therefore simulate in her classroom a scientific microsociety, if she wants the use of knowledge to be an economical way of asking good questions and settling disputes and if she wants language to be a tool for mastering situations of formulation and mathematical proofs to be a means of convincing classmates.
>
> (Brousseau 1997: 23)

Such an approach involved designing situations in which the very nature of the problem provokes the invention of new mathematical knowledge, thus 'backgrounding' the role of the teacher. In the USA the work of the radical constructivists in the 1980s and 1990s also pointed towards the power of students to construct mathematical knowledge for themselves, almost without the need for a teacher.[3]

Although there are subtle differences in viewpoints between the work in France, the work in the UK, and the work in the United States – differences which often relate to views about what mathematics is – nowadays most researchers would agree that in the mathematics classroom 'there is no discovery unless the discoverer has well-developed perspectives, in terms of both language and experienced imaginations of what he or she is going to hunt for, or better – of what he or she is going to make of an object' (Bauersfeld 1995: 279). What Bauersfeld calls well-developed perspectives, relates to ways of seeing, ways of knowing and ways of theorizing. In other words students are not likely to learn what could be called scientific mathematical concepts through engaging with problem situations alone, however carefully these have been designed or engineered. This suggests that classrooms should become knowledge-creating communities with questioning and inquiry being central aspects of this process, and language playing a crucial role in this respect. Nowadays the importance of students being part of a wider community of mathematics learners is acknowledged both by those who are working within a socio-cultural framework and by those who have shifted from a constructivist to a social constructivist frame.[4] This explicitly recognizes the impact of culture on learning, in other words the importance of students being part of a group of people who are actively solving mathematical problems, talking about mathematical ideas and using mathematical tools.

Students as creative and constructive problem solvers

As discussed in Chapter 3 students struggle to find ways to solve problems and this involves using whatever tools they have available, where the idea of tools includes both mathematical tools and symbols and the medium being used, such as paper, pencil or calculator. Consider the following problem, which is usually classified as an 'algebra' problem and is the type of problem which is often used to introduce students to algebra in school:

The Rectangular Field Problem

The perimeter of a field measures 102 metres. The length of the field is twice as much as the width of the field. How much does the length of the field measure? How much does the width of the field measure?

When this problem was presented to primary and secondary students in Mexico and the UK,[5] some students solved this problem using a 'trial-and-refinement' approach. Here the student runs the problem for successive values of appropriate variables:

Well, I tried 40, it was 120 . . . so I knew it must be smaller than that . . . in the 30s . . . and when I tried 36 and it was 108 . . . I knew it couldn't be 35 . . . so it must be 34 . . .

Other students used a whole/parts approach. Here the student relates a part quantity to a whole quantity in order to work from the given whole to the unknown part:

I did 102 divided by 6 . . . I just did two of the lengths to make it sensible . . . I just thought there must be two of those in one length . . .

When the problem was presented to vocational engineering students some students used a more visual approach by making a sketch similar to the following:

Problems such as the rectangular field problem were designed to introduce an algebraic approach such as

Let the width of the field = X metres.
Let the length of the field = L metres.

$$\text{Then } L = 2X - (1)$$
$$\text{and } 2L + 2X = 102 - (2)$$
$$\text{So by substituting (1) in (2)}$$
$$4X + 2X = 102$$
$$6X = 102$$
$$X = 17 \text{ metres.}$$

How then can a teacher deal with these multiple problem-solving approaches which students are likely to bring to the solution of a problem?

Teacher and tools

The role of the teacher can be conceptualized as one of introducing students to new mathematical tools, with an awareness of the ways in which each student already brings with them a portfolio of tools to any problem-solving situation. If the aim is to introduce students to a new mathematical tool (for example multiplication, linear equations) it is important to be aware that students are already likely to be able to solve any presented problem with an alternative tool (for example repeated addition, trial and refinement).

An emphasis on the relative effectiveness of particular mathematical tools allows us to critically consider the role of digital tools and whether or not they are likely to replace non-digital tools. For example, will digital graph-plotting packages ultimately replace paper-and-pencil graphs? Will computer algebra systems ultimately replace paper-based calculus? Will calculators ultimately replace mental calculations? As soon as we begin to ask questions like these it becomes clear that it is more helpful to ask questions such as, what does a paper-and-pencil graph offer? What does a graph-plotting package offer? This moves away from unhelpful polarization of digital and non-digital tools to a realization that some non-digital tools have lasting value, whereas others (such as the algorithm for calculating a square root) fade with time. This suggests that it is important to consider the potential affordance of a particular tool in the context of the problems being solved. What does a particular tool offer and what does it do for you?

Interestingly, the question about when and how to use mathematical tools in schools is different from when and how to use mathematical tools in the workplace. This is because in school the emphasis is on learning about particular mathematical knowledge, learning about particular mathematical tools, whereas in the workplace the emphasis is on solving particular problems.

An illustrative vignette – learning statistics in the primary school

The most powerful way of introducing students to new mathematical ideas is to work creatively with a whole class so that students become collectively aware of the potential of new mathematical tools: new mathematical knowledge. Superficially this might seem like the traditional model of teaching in which a teacher transmits knowledge, because there may be occasions in which the teacher does introduce new mathematical tools when standing at the front of the class. However, these are only occasions and for most of the time students will be working on solving problems for themselves. Throughout the lesson the teacher can shift between the following roles:

- More knowledgeable other
- Co-constructor of knowledge
- Vicarious participant.

In order to illustrate this way of working I use an example from a class in which a primary-school teacher, Simon Mills, found a way of introducing 8–9-year-old students to statistical ideas. Simon teaches in a primary school in South Bristol. This is not a school in a privileged middle-class area, quite the contrary. Simon developed this work through his partnership in the Inter-Active Education Project[6] and as he explained: 'A major focus of the project from my perspective was to focus the children on the function of charts and to encourage them to think about the features of charts, which enable them to be useful in helping us think mathematically'. To develop a framework for this study Simon analysed the mathematics, the numeracy and the ICT curriculum documents[7] and synthesized this analysis into a diagram (Figure 4.1). As this diagram shows, ideas related to data handling are specified in the National Numeracy Strategy (NNC), the ICT curriculum (ICT) and Attainment Target 1 (MA 1) and Attainment target 4 (MA 4) of the mathematics curriculum.

Simon recognized that he needed to find a rich problem in order to contextualize this work and decided to use a problem situation which had been developed by Janet Ainley (1996) and colleagues – an investigation of the distribution of different coloured smarties in a smartie tube. He formulated the following starting-point question: '*Does every tube of Smarties contain the same number of each colour? How many tubes of Smarties would I have to buy to get a fair share of my favourite orange ones?*' The work took place over eight 1-hour sessions spread over two weeks. The students used the spreadsheet Excel as a mathematical tool, together with paper-and-pencil charts and

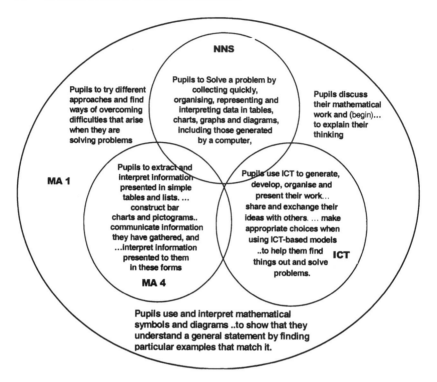

Figure 4.1 Simon Mills's analysis of data handling in curriculum documents

graphs. Simon also used an interactive whiteboard as a basis for creating a community of inquiry in the classroom.

The following is an excerpt from an article which Simon wrote for *Micromath*:

> The teaching sequence began with a series of whole class and group discussions. In pairs the children explored a collection of 'real' charts presenting data in different formats. Not all the chart types were familiar to the children, this was important, in light of my long term aims which were to explore the function of charts, and to encourage the children to think together about those features which make them useful in real life. During their exploration the children were encouraged to view the materials as they might a diagram or piece of text from a book, and consider 5 main questions
>
> • What was the chart about?
> • Who might have made the chart and why?
> • Who might find it useful?

- How useful was the chart?
- And what features of the charts enabled them to make these decisions?

As they worked together I supported their discussion helping to identify chart features that enabled us to make sense of them. Children were encouraged to discard charts they found problematic, but asked to present their reasons for discarding them.

In review a PowerPoint presentation, which included the charts we had discussed, was used to focus class discussion, and help gather together the children's views about 'what makes a good chart?' This type of process is common in the context of literacy sessions. Teachers often work with students to evaluate and record the features of texts, which are later used as prompts in guided or shared writing sessions. Children use the features of say a 'good instructional text' as a model to help organise and structure their own writing and as a checklist for evaluating their completed outcomes. In this context it provided a vehicle to use and apply the language conventions associated with charts and graphs in a class discussion, for example title, axis, label, bar, column and so on. This discussion also allowed us to identify the types of charts presented and to discuss what possible uses they might have. This introductory activity also elicited invaluable formative assessment data. The children had a very clear understanding of simple frequency tables, tally charts, Carroll and Venn Diagrams and how they worked. They had some understanding of bar and line charts which used discontinuous data, and were able to visually interpret pie charts by comparing the relative sizes of their segments. The group were very critical of pictograms, as representational devices, and raised a number of issues which lead to a great deal of discussion regarding the importance of how we present data to an audience, if it is to be meaningful. When I later considered the charts discarded by children, they were as I'd predicted those which presented data continuously. Discussion revealed that these chart types were completely unfamiliar to the group.

For the sessions which followed, I used an interactive whiteboard and a range of both commercially and freely available Interactive Teaching Programs (ITPs), to explore methods for data collection, and presentation. Again we referred to our charted features of 'good charts' identified earlier. We also spent time 'thinking together' about chart titles and axis labels, which would help our readers understand what our data was about.

These classroom based activities, were followed by a guided investigational activity, based on an idea presented by Janet Ainley

(1996: 28). For this series of activities, we moved to the ICT suite. The children were each given a tube of Smarties. I told them my favourite sweets were Smarties, particularly the orange ones. I had noticed though, that their never seemed to be a fair share of these in any of the tubes I bought. The children were asked to work in pairs and to help me investigate whether this was true. They were introduced to Microsoft Excel^M and asked to construct a frequency table to represent the number of each colour Smartie in their tube. It was interesting observing the children as they sorted and counted their sweets.

Some grouped their smarties by colour, and counted these entering the results into the spreadsheet. Others arranged their smarties into columns, similar in form to bar charts and pictograms, comparing them before counting them. (see Figures 4.2 and 4.3)

Some children began exploring the software environment unprompted. The children had used several other Microsoft applications in the past, and were familiar with the use of 'Wizards' as tools and templates. They were also aware that usually they needed to highlight by 'drag and drop' in order to use features within these applications. I noticed that one pair of students had begun using the chart wizard feature to explore independently the different types of chart they could present using Excel. I decided to draw on this opportunity, and the following day encouraged one child to present what he had learned to the rest of the class.

(Mills 2004: 19)

As Simon explained in this article students worked in pairs at the computer, but this pair-work was framed by whole-class work in which Simon sometimes taught from the front and sometimes invited other students to share what they knew. Sometimes this sharing was about mathematics and sometimes about how to use Excel. In all these situations Simon and the other students in the class participated together in the discussion, with Simon entering into a dialogue with students as they jointly co-constructed knowledge:

Simon:	It's a title it needs so what title?
All:	Pie chart.
Simon:	Yes ... it's a little bit more than a pie chart.
All:	A pie chart of smarties ... frequency ... pie chart of ... Year 4.
Simon:	Pie chart of Year 4's favourite smarties.

This discussion of the title of the chart was carried out by the whole class and Simon typed in the pupil's suggestions on the interactive whiteboard. As Simon explains:

Well, I think the role of the interactive whiteboard changed as the project went on. I think initially it was a modelling device. It was a means by which I could demonstrate and model what children were doing. I think what it became later was a window and a way to view what children were actually doing and had learnt.

The attention to the titles of each graph was evident in the students' final work which was produced as a whole-class collective work (see Figure 4.4).

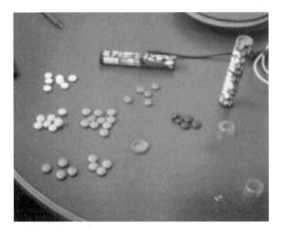

Figure 4.2 Grouping Smarties in colour

Figure 4.3 Towards a bar chart

Overall Simon's approach within this sequence of lessons can be characterized by:

- pre-planning which involved choosing a starting-point problem and complexifying the area to be taught (see for example Figure 4.1); and
- contingent teaching which opportunistically used what the students brought to the lesson to extend their learning.

For example, Simon had not planned to introduce pie charts but when these were introduced into the lesson through the explorations of one student he invited this student to share the ideas with the whole class. As this student showed the whole class how to construct a pie chart from data he also explained how to make the colour of each pie match the smartie colour it was representing. This powerful idea was taken up by all the students in the class. Subsequently Simon went on to use the students' pie-chart work to discuss percentages (some students had discovered that it is possible to place percentages onto an Excel pie chart) and also fractions. He also used this opportunity to emphasize the difference between a bar chart and a pie chart.

Students owned the 'smarties' problem and delighted in producing their own work as illustrated in Figure 4.4. Analysis of video data shows how Simon subtly influenced what the students discovered by creating appropriate mathematical perspectives, drawing on the students' discoveries to introduce new mathematical ideas such as percentages and fractions.

yellow	7	11	10	8	10	9	0	11	8	6	
green	8	3	6	5	10	4	0	7	5	3	
purple	4	5	6	7	5	3	1	4	9	2	This is some data that
oranges	4	10	4	4	3	3	4	3	4	2	we collected.The first
pink	10	5	5	7	3	5	3	6	4	2	two is Shannie's and
blue	5	2	5	4	4	4	9	3	3	9	max's.The others are
brown	5	7	6	2	4	10	0	7	7	3	other peoples data.
red	0	3	3	7	6	5	4	6	8	4	The totals are at the
	43	46	45	44	45	43	21	47	48	31	bottom.

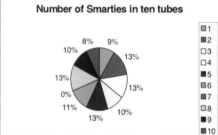

Number of Smarties in ten tubes

8% 9%
10%
13%
13%
13%
0%
11%
13% 10%
13%

■1
■2
□3
□4
■5
■6
■7
□8
■9
■10

This is the pie chart for 10 tubes of Smarties. Look at the data at the top we put it in to a Pie

We started of with opening are Smartie tube and sorted them in to the colours.We counted how many of each colour there was. When we counted the colours we typed in the names of all eight and then we put are data in.We collected data from other groups and found out that they do not all have the same amount. We found out that you can not get the same amount.Max's tube didn't have any Reds at all but Shannie had all the colours that should be in the tube. The question was false. We would defently like to be able to do more with Publisher and Exel.

Max's and Shannie

We tried to get it equal by collecting other peoples data and putting there data into a pie chart. Look at the title if you are not sure what it's about.

This work was carried out in 2004 and Simon reworked the design initiative with a new class of Year 4 pupils in 2005 for a Teacher's TV[8] programme which can be downloaded from http://www.teachers.tv. During that academic year (2004–5) the school was inspected by OFSTED[9] who said the following about the culture of the school:

> Pupils enter the school with very low levels of literacy and unusually poorly developed communication skills, many pupils have a very restricted vocabulary, listening skills are underdeveloped and understanding poor ... The majority of pupils use single words or short phrases, seldom answering in full sentences. Much of their speech is inaudible to the whole class [... not possessing the vocabulary or confidence to make longer contributions].

and the following about Simon Mills's teaching:

> Nearly all lessons have good pace. This is a significant factor in engaging the interest and involvement of all pupils. This was evident in a very good Year 4 mathematics lesson where the wide range of strategies and changing between them, engaged pupils' interest and ensured they concentrated well and developed increasing understanding of the concept of symmetry.
>
> A good link in numeracy was seen in Year 4, when the teacher introduced branching databases for sorting geometric shapes.
>
> Mathematics programmes were used appropriately during lessons by pupils and by teachers for class demonstrations on their interactive whiteboards.
>
> Older pupils have positive attitudes to their learning; they are used to talking to their partners about ideas they have to solve problems.

Concluding remarks

A strong claim which runs throughout this book is that students do not spontaneously enter new mathematical worlds. In the earlier example Simon constructed a situation in which students entered the world of data handling and statistics. Students brought their existing and informal knowledge to the situation and Simon drew on this knowledge, but also systematically presented students with new knowledge. Another important aspect of Simon's work is that although he drew upon students' expertise and respected what they knew he also explicitly intended to confront them with new mathematical knowledge. Sometimes this was pre-planned and other times he opportunistically introduced unplanned ideas, for example fractions and percentages. Within this community students also emerged as 'knowledgeable others'.

The example from Simons's class shows how digital tools have opened up new ways for students of all ages to access and engage with a wide range of mathematical ideas. Working with the digital spreadsheet students were able to produce and manipulate graphs in a way which would have been hardly possible with paper and pencil. It is also likely that they wrote more with the digital tool than they would have done on paper, and certainly as Figure 4.4 illustrates they were focusing on mathematical ideas and not on spelling. The interactive whiteboard was also a digital tool which was used to make visible the learning and thinking of the whole class.

This example also illustrates the way in which digital tools are only part of the wide range of tools which are an important part of any mathematical activity. They do not replace the old tools such as paper and pencil and books, but they can add to them in substantial ways. Simon also worked with students to enable them to become aware of the different affordances of graphical representations. 'Bar charts are good for ...', 'pie charts are good for ...'. This awareness of the affordances of each tool was an explicit aspect of the whole framing of the sequence of lessons.

Possibly more important than anything I have discussed already is Simon's respect for his students and his belief that they would be able to engage with challenging mathematical ideas: *'I want the children to believe in themselves and to believe that they can do what it is that we set out to achieve.'* This respect for students has to be the starting point for all teaching for learning mathematics. It is very important for young people to know that their existing knowledge (the old mathematical tools as it were) are being valued by their teacher and their classmates. Rejection or undervaluing of their previous experience is likely to lead to alienation and possible disruptive or subversive behaviour. Discontinuities between the culture of the home and the school and mismatches in communities of practice between home and school can be an explanatory factor in school failure.[10]

We all know from our own personal experience that if what we offer is continuously undervalued by a group then we are likely to leave the group. However, valuing what students already know and using this to support them to leap into new knowledge worlds is very different from reifying what they know to the point where they are likely to see no purpose in learning anything new. In fact reification of students' existing informal knowledge could be seen as a way of maintaining the power relationship between a teacher and students.

Notes

1. See for example Hart et al. (1981).
2. For example the textbook scheme SMP 11–16 which was widely used in England throughout the 1980s.
3. See for example Von Glaserfield (2003).
4. See Cobb and Bauersfeld (1995).
5. For further discussion of this work see Rojano (1996) and Sutherland and Rojano (1993).
6. See www.interactiveeduction.ac.uk.
7. See www.qca.org.uk.
8. Teacher's TV is a new digital chanel which has been developed for teachers; http://www.teachers.tv/home.do. See Mills et al. (2005) for a Teacher's TV programme on Simon Mills's work on data handling.
9. Office for Standards in Education; http:/www.ofsted.gov.uk.
10. For further discussion of this see Scribner and Cole (1981).

5 Teaching and Learning as Reciprocal Activity

If the teacher doesn't have too many limitations, you know, say for example you wanted to insert a Clipart from a different file and the teacher originally knew, you know ... this is the way you should do it, and then you said, 'No I know another way to do it to get better images and stuff'. Then a good teacher like Miss Paterson would let you do this. Okay? And then *she would take on your information that you inputted into the lesson. She learns from you and you learn from her. So it's like a two-way system.* It's not like some teachers who, you know, pound it into you, try to just get information into you, they don't get anything back, that's a bad teaching manner, I don't like that type of teaching at all when the teacher just gives you information and says, 'Write it down' bla bla bla 'This is it. Revise from it'. That's not good teaching at all. Good teaching is when the teacher asks for questions from the class and answers the questions that the kids give, you know. That's good teaching. But when they just give you information and that's it, they don't answer questions, they don't let you involve yourself in the lesson, that's not a good type of teaching, that's really bad teaching.

(Huw, 13-year-old boy in South Wales; Screen Play Project)[1]

What is teaching?

This chapter is concerned with examining the relationship between teaching and learning mathematics. The starting point for discussion is represented by the above quotation, which was expressed by one of the young people who participated in the Screen Play Project. Huw expresses very succinctly his ideas about good teaching and bad teaching. Good teaching, for Huw, is a two-way system, a sharing of knowledge. Bad teaching is when a teacher tries to 'pound information into you'. But although it is recognized that good teaching is not about telling, that good teaching is not about a conduit metaphor of communicating knowledge, moving away from such dominant practices does not always seem to be easy. And interestingly, as I shall discuss further in Chapter 9, we are beginning to understand how imitation (which incorrectly is often viewed hand in hand with direct teaching) does actually play an important role in the learning process.

The aim throughout this book is to present a range of case studies which exemplify the complexity of teaching and learning. The aim is not to present one model but a range of practices. The aim is also to present tools for teachers to examine teaching and learning in their own classrooms. These tools are both theoretical (for example socio-cultural theory) and concrete (for example the use of digital video, diagnostic assessment, narratives of classroom practices).

Following on from the vignette of Simon Mills's work (Chapter 4) this chapter focuses on the ways in which a teacher can create a classroom culture in which there is an emergence of what has been called a 'consensual domain' (Bauersfeld 1995). This does not mean that all students are focusing on the same processes or constructing the same knowledge, but that through dialogue, actions and interactions a sort of common knowledge emerges. The focus is on the collective construction of knowledge in which 'the teacher and students jointly develop and deepen a specific and differentiated language game, based on taken-as-shared experiences, activities and objects, there will be better chances for a sufficient mutual understanding and an effective interaction' (Bauersfeld 1995: 279).

Communities of inquiry

Whereas Chapter 4 opened up the idea of digital tools for teaching and learning mathematics, this chapter focuses on the use of non-digital whiteboards. Two detailed cases are presented in order to discuss and analyse the idea of classrooms as communities of inquiry. The first draws on the work of the research project 'Developing Algebraic Activity in a Community of Inquirers' (Brown et al. 2001). This project followed on from Laurinda Brown's (Brown 1990; Brown and Coles 1999, 2003) earlier work on developing ways of introducing the algebraic language to 11–16-year-old students. I have chosen this example for two reasons. First because it shows the possibility of algebra emerging as part of whole-class mathematical activity, where algebraic symbolism and algebraic processes are inextricably linked. Second, this example illustrates a possible way of using a (non-digital) whiteboard as a tool for collective classroom work. The second case draws on the work of the InterActive Education Project[2] and also shows how a (non-digital) whiteboard can be used as a collective common memory space which enables students and teacher to build knowledge together.

Shared mathematical working spaces – learning algebra

Introduction

In this section I discuss the way in which Alf Coles uses a whiteboard to create a 'community of inquiry' for learning algebra. Alf usually works with students over a number of lessons on a complex problem with homework being an integral part of this process. He uses the rotating whiteboard at the front of the class as a dynamic and shared workspace (see for example Figure 5.1). In this lesson students were working on a problem which involved them in generating rules for the areas of squares that had been constructed on dotted paper. Students had been encouraged to work on both the specific and the general and to generate their own conjectures about general rules. They were invited to offer their contributions to the whole class through writing on the common whiteboard. In the previous lesson students were working on the questions (which were constructed by them):

- Is there a pattern to how to work out the area?
- Can you predict which areas are possible and which are impossible?
- Can I be organized in the way I draw the squares?
- Can I be sure that I've got them all?

The class had already found that the squares could be oriented in several ways which they called 'normal squares' or 'squares on angles'.

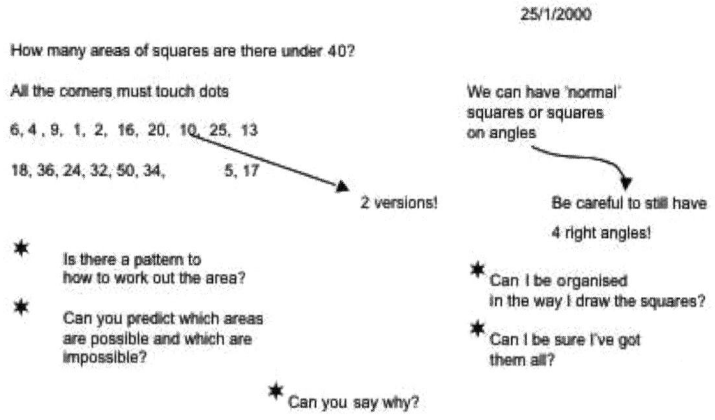

Figure 5.1 Whiteboard at the beginning of the lesson

Getting organized – emphasizing structure

Alf started the lesson by emphasizing what he called 'getting organized' (observations of Alf show that he often emphasizes the need to be organized, which in some respects relates to the idea of mathematical structure).

> *T:*   At the end of last time one question people were working on was ... *can I be organized in the way I draw the squares* and ... in particular can I do it *so that I can be sure I have got them all* ... and as I said last time that is the way I would like to begin with today and see where that leads us ... so ... can we be organized in the way we draw the squares and can we therefore be *sure* that we have got them all ... [Alf then moved the whiteboard so that there was a clean area to work on].
>
> *T:*   I am going to ... in a moment ... to ask someone to come up and draw a beginning square in a way to be organized ... but I want us to think about it just for a moment ... when we say can we be sure that we are going to be organized ... what do we mean ... can someone *say what does it mean to say we have got them all* ... Mike ...

As the lesson evolved it became apparent that the teacher was asking the class to develop a systematic way of representing squares and their areas, with the purpose of ensuring that all possible patterns had been taken into account. Alf was drawing attention to mathematical structure by asking students to anticipate the emergent system for representing all the areas:

> *T:*   I am going to ask someone to come up and draw a beginning shape ... but if we are thinking about what areas we can make ... you can't be organized thinking about those areas ... you can't be organized by saying ... I am going to draw this one because it is the next biggest area ... cos that's what we are trying to test out ... we are trying to test out if we do have the next biggest area ... so you can't say this is the next one in my pattern because it is the next biggest one ... that will hopefully become clearer once we begin ...

Alf then invited the students to test out their ideas by drawing 'a square with some system' on the whiteboard:

> *T:*   Would someone like to come up and draw *a square with some system* that they have got ... some way of being organized in finding the squares ... *in finding all of them* ... OK Sam.

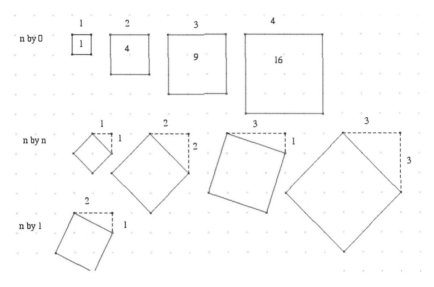

Figure 5.2 The emerging notation system

Sam came to the board and drew the first square in Row 1 (see Figure 5.2). Alf's comments emphasized the need to anticipate the system which was being developed:

> *T:*   I want ... in fact Sam have you got a second one because in order to see your system we have to see a second one ... OK can someone else come and draw the next one ... the reason can't be that it is the next biggest one ... because that's what we're trying to test ... I want another shape with a system of being organized which isn't about that it's the next biggest one ...

A girl came to the whiteboard and drew the second square in Row 1:

> *T:*   OK ... if that makes sense someone should be able to draw the next one ... if this is a system ... someone should be able to follow it ... could someone else draw the next one in the sequence.

Another girl came to the whiteboard and drew the third square in Row 1:

> *T:*   Should we have one more in the sequence ... if Candia's sequence makes sense everyone else should be able to continue that sequence on ...

Another girl came to the whiteboard and drew the fourth square ... (at this stage only the four squares in Row 1 (Figure 5.2) appeared with no other writing surrounding them).

Through this collective work on the whiteboard all the class could see and become aware of a system for generating squares and their areas. The row of squares had been generated by the students themselves and Alf continued to ask the students to explain the system being generated. As the squares were generated many students said things as they looked at the first row of squares *'If you have a diamond it would be a hard ...', 'It is ... organize ... goes 1 ... the next one 2 ... the next one 3 ... the next one 4 ...'.*

Having set up an activity in which all students were actively involved in seeing, saying and doing Alf 'nudged' the class towards the idea of finding a systematic way of labelling the rows of squares which were being generated. In some sense the Alf was directing the class, but it was the students themselves who were generating the ideas:

Anne:	It is ... organize ... goes 1 ... the next one 2 ... the next one 3 ... the next one 4 ...
T:	So what you are talking about is a way we could actually label these squares and talk about them ... OK ... yes ...
Anne:	The first one is 1 by 1 ... the second one is 2 by 2 ... 3 by 3 ... 4 by 4 ...
T:	Anyone got a comment on Anne's way of talking about these squares ... any one else got a way ... OK so Anne wants to call this a 1 by 1 ... square ... OK ... anyone got another way of talking about these things ...
Boy:	2 by 4.

It seems as if Alf was anticipating that the suggested labelling system would not readily generalize to other rows of squares:

T:	OK ... certainly in some sense that's 1 2 3 and 4 ... I think calling it a 1 by 1 may get us into difficulties ... but we'll see when we get diamond ones ... we'll see if we can find a way of labelling both of them ... Gill.
Gill:	You could say like 2 dots and then 3 dots and 4 dots and 5 dots ...

At this point there was more discussion of potential labelling systems for the first row of squares but Alf 'suspended' for a while the labelling of the squares in row 1 and instead invited the students to generate the second row of squares so that they themselves could become aware (through seeing) of the need for a more general notation system than that which had already been proposed. After some discussion a girl came to the board and drew the first shape of the next row (Figure 5.2). A boy then drew the second square of the second row (all students were also drawing in their own books).

T:	It is much more difficult to draw the next one ... OK ... could we try to follow his system ... so he has maybe got a system of being organized there ... the test of it is if someone could draw the next one in the sequence which they could agree with...

Another student came to the whiteboard and drew the third square in the second row (Figure 5.2). This third square was actually not the third in the sequence being generated for this row. Many of the students in the class were able to see this and at this point another girl came up and drew what she thought was the third square in this sequence:

Boy:	It could be like that because you could ... because he went from umm ... cos he went from ... Jane done 2 ... then Craig missed out 5 ... done 8 ... miss out 10 ... the next one ... go to 13 ...
T:	OK what are we trying to test for here ... what are we trying to look at ... we are trying to be organized for what purposes here ... why are we trying to be organized ... so we can find all of the areas ... so our system can't make ... shouldn't mention the areas ... our system should be just based on the shape ... because if we base our system on the areas ... we...
Gill:	I think Candia's is next because if ... [inaudible] two dots on a slant and then 3 dots and then 4 dots ... and then...
T:	So could someone find a way ... so as Anne had a way of labelling this one could someone find a way...

Alf then returned to the idea of labelling the rows and a student suggested using the notation n by n for the second row:

David:	n by n
T:	Why n by n, David?
David:	Because the five ... [inaudible]...

David came up and labelled 1 and 1 on the whiteboard (see Figure 5.2):

T:	1 by 1 ... so the next one in the sequence ... can you do the next one?

David wrote 2 by 2 on the whiteboard. At this point Alf asked the students to label row 1:

T: OK ... so this is quite exciting ... so this is 1 by 1 ... 2 by 2 ... 3 by 3 ... *according to that system what would this be* ... could we label these ones ... in the same way as we labelled those ones [pointing to first row].
David: *n by 0*
T: n by 0 ... go on David why ... can anyone see why this should be the *n by 0 family* ... Angela.
Angela: Cos you don't need to draw another triangle to make a whole square ... so it's already a square.
T: So it's already a square ... so I'm just going 1 across and no down ... and then I'm going 2 across ... and 3 across and then 4 across ... OK so we've got *a n by 0 family and an n by n family* ... so could someone think what would be the next one ... so I'm not sure ... we might think about reorganizing these in a moment, given David's nice way of thinking about these ... could someone give me another family we could try ... so I could be organized. Here ... Gill ... oh you are going to draw one ... right come and draw one ... can you say what family it is going to be?

The lesson continued with students generating the first square of row 3, the emerging labelling system and also writing 'n by 2' and 'n by 3' besides what would become row 4 and row 5 respectively.

Discussion – shared working space

Within this example I have focused on one lesson in detail as this provides a basis for discussing how the teacher, Alf Coles, found ways of supporting students to develop meaning for the objects and processes of algebra. This lesson illustrates that for Alf, working with students on the language and notation aspect of algebra is an integral part of the communication within the classroom. In this sense 'language aspects of algebra' are not separated from 'approaches to algebra'. Alf made available to the class his own struggle with language to express the complex idea of developing a representational system which could be used as a means of justifying that all possible 'squares' have been found. In this class students were also confident about expressing their half-formed ideas in language, which suggests that the teacher was an important facilitator in this respect. The dialogue between teacher and students, and the actions of the students as they worked at the whiteboard were both aspects of the way in which mathematical meaning was constructed in this classroom. Analysis of the transcript of the lesson shows how the whole class participated in the joint construction of the system for generating all the squares and how the symbolic representation emerged as an integral part of developing awareness of the system.

Alf could not have predicted in advance how this particular class would respond to this particular problem. But his experience as a teacher enabled him to work contingently on what the students brought to the lesson. He was confident that the particular problem situation, worked on over several lessons, would lead to rich mathematical work.

In this lesson we can see that although the teacher orchestrated the work of the whole class his ideas were developed from the students in an ongoing organic way. Thus the use of symbolic algebra emerged from a situation that was meaningful for the students, a situation in which students were likely to be focusing their attention on the same aspect of a problem through the collective use of the whiteboard. Alf both respected what the students were offering and at the same time intended to introduce the students to new ways of symbolizing in algebra.

Shared mathematical working spaces – learning functions and graphs

Introduction

In the previous example Alf Coles used a rotating whiteboard to keep track of the history of the collective work of the class. This enabled the work of the previous lesson to be available in the subsequent lesson. Rachel Zewde[3] has developed a different yet also powerful use of a fixed whiteboard. The board in Rachel's classroom covered a large horizontal space at the front of her class, which allowed for the representation of collective work of the class (see Figure 5.3).

This example shows how Rachel used the whiteboard to work with the whole class to build up a collective understanding of the properties of linear functions. She did this over a period of four lessons by presenting students with a range of examples of linear functions, encouraging them to notice their properties and then experiment themselves with a graphics calculator. Rachel started the third lesson by spending some time establishing the properties of the graph y = x, namely the fact that it passes through the origin and that the x and y coordinates are always equal at any point along the line. Working with the whole class she asked questions in order to encourage them to notice these properties for themselves, for example:

Rachel: Maybe half the class have memorized that y = x but what does it mean in terms of the x numbers and y numbers?

and

Rachel: If I picked a point on that line [marks point 2,2] what's that point got to do with the equation y = x?

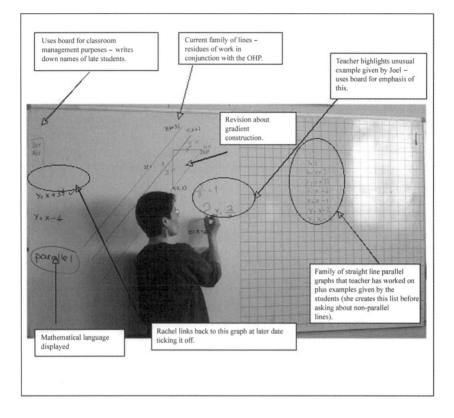

Figure 5.3   A snapshot in time of Rachel's use of whiteboard space. Here Rachel is writing down and emphasizing a function suggested by John

Rachel used both the whiteboard and an overhead projector (which projected from a Texas Instruments calculator). Using these tools Rachel began to introduce the idea of linear functions which were not parallel to functions of the form $y = x + a$. Here the whiteboard became a tool for the collective recording of whole-class work (Figure 5.3):

> *Rachel:*   Who could give me a line that will not be parallel? ... John?
>
> *John:*   Y equals 2 over x
>
> *Rachel:*   Right, I'm going to put that aside. Did you try investigating these ones?
>
> *John:*   No.
>
> *Rachel:*   If you want to try that John, something will change completely so I'm going to leave that aside. That is almost too difficult but you'll see why if you try that. It certainly would not be parallel so you've answered my questions right but

you'll find it's not a straight line. OK, so pretend John's never happened, although it's a very good idea. Something a little bit more like that but I don't want it to be parallel. Andrew?

Andrew: y = −x add 4.

Although John's response to Rachel's question about a function which is not parallel to y = x + a was correct, it was not the type of response which Rachel had anticipated. What is interesting here is the way in which Rachel showed that she valued the response by writing it centrally on the board, while at the same time focusing the class discussion in the direction she had intended (see Figure 5.3).

Other students suggested functions which are not parallel to y = x and Rachel added these to the list on the board (y = −2x and y = 5x + 3).

After this opening session of the lesson the students were asked to use their graphics calculators to construct a set of functions which were not parallel to y = x + a. John now had an opportunity to try out his suggested function y = 2/x and as this function was drawn the following interchange took place between John and Mike:

John: The gradient gets steeper and steeper.
Mike: What?
John: The gradients gets steeper and steeper.

The whole-class work had provoked John to think about investigating functions of the form y = 2/x and then work with a graphics calculator had enabled him to pursue this line of investigation. It would have been much more difficult for John to carry out this investigation if he had been using paper-and-pencil graphs.

Discussion

In this way of working with a static whiteboard what seems to be important is the way in which Rachel drew on the work of members of the class to build up a collective knowledge-building community, with students' work being placed in the collective working space. In contrast to Alf's class it was Rachel who usually placed the students' work on the board, although occasionally it would be the students themselves who came out to the front of the class to draw their own functions. The use of graphics calculators added another dimension to students' work and enabled them to investigate functions which would have been difficult to investigate with paper-and-pencil graphical tools. Interestingly the small display of the graphics screen did not preclude the possibilities of student collaboration. For example, when John and Mike were working at the same table with their own individual calculators they did show each other their calculator screens on several occasions and John keyed in to Mike's calculator when trying to show him what to do. It is interesting that despite the fact that these two students had not been told to work as a pair there was a substantial amount of task-related cross-communication and collaborative talk between them.

Concluding remarks

Alf and Rachel approach the teaching of mathematics in different ways, but they both exploit the potential of whiteboards to create a community of inquiry in which students collectively work on mathematics. In both examples students behave in unpredictable ways and the teacher makes choices about how to manage these situations. In this sense their behaviour is contingent on the students' behaviour. Rachel chose to write the 'unexpected non-linear' function on the board, and this seems to have given John permission to carry on with an investigation of this function on the graphic calculator. Interestingly John was a student who was often disaffected by school, yet with this work on functions he made more progress than any other student in the class. This may be because work with graphics calculators enabled him to investigate for himself his non-standard ideas. Use of the graphics calculators seems to have enabled the class to be more experimental with functions and graphs than Rachel had expected.[4]

In Alf's class students were explicitly encouraged to generate their own questions and these were used as a basis of working from lesson to lesson. The rotating whiteboard enabled time to be represented in a way which was not possible with the static board. In Alf's class most of the writing on the board was carried out by the students themselves and this provided a shared focus of attention for the whole class.

In this chapter I have focused on the use of the more traditional non-digital whiteboard because the potential of this tool is not always realized in mathematics classrooms. Unless we understand more about the importance of tools for representing collective whole-class work, the digital interactive whiteboard is not likely to be fully exploited. These cases illustrate the power and possibilities of shared working spaces which make visible the mathematical thinking of the whole class. As with the work of Simon Mills discussed in Chapter 4 they also illustrate the ways in which a teacher can both respect and draw upon students' existing knowledge while at the same time leading students into new mathematical knowledge worlds.

Notes

1. See Facer et al. (2003).
2. A fuller discussion of the whole approach is discussed in Brown and Coles (2001).
3. This example is taken from the work of the InterActive Education Project (www.interactiveeducation.ac.uk).
4. For further discussion of this work see Godwin and Sutherland (2004).

6 Digital Tools for Learning Mathematics

Mathematics and computer programming

Mathematics was one of the earlier subjects to make use of the computer in the classroom. This is not surprising because the first digital computers were primarily developed to solve differential equations and had evolved from Babbage's automatic calculating machine.[1] In the early 1980s many people (including myself) were convinced that computer programming could provide a valuable way into learning mathematics.[2] I became interested in the relationship between computer programming and learning mathematics when I was teaching mathematics to post-16 students who were studying a vocational computing course. Many of these students were also studying an advanced-level mathematics course and I began to think that they might be able to use their knowledege of computer programming to help them learn some of the mathematical ideas which they were finding difficult, and in particular algebra. My first job in the late 1960s had been as a computer programmer and I was personally aware of the potential links between mathematics and computer programming. This led me to become interested in the Logo programming language which my own children were learning in primary school as part of the Chiltern Logo Project.[3] This also led to the conceptualization of the Logo Mathematics Project,[4] a project whose main aim was to increase understanding of how Logo might provide an environment for the experiential learning of mathematics. In particular as part of work on a doctoral thesis I investigated the ways in which Logo programming could be used to transform the learning of algebra.[5]

I explain this history because it has influenced my views about using computers for teaching and learning mathematics. Working with Logo strengthened my belief that young people can learn to use computers in ways which were previously restricted to the domain of university students. Working with Logo also convinced me that learning programming can impact on students' learning of mathematics.

In Chapter 3 I presented the case of a primary student, Alistair, that illustrates the ways in which computer programming can impact on learning mathematics. Anthony was also a student who developed an understanding of algebra from Basic programming. Anthony had not met algebraic symbols in school mathematics, yet when asked the question 'which is larger 2n or

$n + 2$?' he responded, 'You can't say that because it wouldn't always be right … if n was 6 that would be 12 … and that would be 8 so that would be right … but if n was one then $2n$ would be 2 and $n = 2$ would be 3'. This response to an item which was only answered correctly by 6 per cent of 14-year-olds in the CSMS study (Küchemann 1981) suggests an appreciation of the second-order relationships between the two expressions $2n$ and $n + 2$. When asked why he was able to answer the interview questions correctly he said, 'It might be partly because of Basic, where I've learned to use things like variables and things … like p is a number and you can use any letter for a number …'.

Anthony was interviewed a year later at age 11, just after he had started secondary school. He said that he was finding school mathematics 'a bit easy at the moment'. He again explained his work at home with Basic:

> In Basic there's quite a lot of maths involved in it. I did a program that calculates your age … it's still a bit faulty at the moment … but what it does you enter your age in years and the date … well just the date and the month that you were born and it calculates the year you were born and how many years and days old you are.

Anthony had learned to use symbols in algebra to transform what he could do, he seemed to have learned the power and potential of algebraic symbols: 'in algebra … in words … you've got to … sometimes … it's quite hard to explain in words'. Interestingly during this first year of secondary school his teacher was concerned that he was never attempting more than the set homework. Like Alistair, whom I discussed in Chapter 3, Anthony was becoming disinterested in school mathematics at secondary school because it did not tap into the expertise which he had developed outside school. His teacher was not aware of this and thus could not respect his emerging knowledge of algebra. Like Alistair he was challenging himself at home to write computer programmes: 'I did a program that calculates your age … it's still a bit faulty at the moment … but what it does you enter in your age in years and the date … well just the date and the month that you were born and it calculates the year you were born and how many years and days old you are'.

At the time of writing this book there is still an enormous gap between the potential represented in this work and what is being realized in mathematics classrooms. The cases of Alistair and Anthony are both examples of boys from middle-class families who, through the intersection of their own interests and their out-of-school culture, were able to learn computer programming and make links between programming and mathematics. In the case of these two boys their learning had been supported by their family and friends. We know from surveys of young people's out-of-school use of computers that only a small minority of them engage in computer programming or related activities and that most of these young people are boys (Kent and

Facer 2004). Whereas this out-of-school potential points to what is possible, it also points to the role of schools and teachers in creating a culture in school for all students who do not have these types of opportunities out of school.

Regrettably Logo programming has not been integrated into the teaching and learning of mathematics in ways which its advocates had hoped. When Logo did become part of the curriculum its use tended to be restricted to a very small part of what was possible. Despite the research evidence[6] which shows that even young students can learn complex programming ideas, the vast majority of teachers did not introduce students to the powerful ideas of Logo, such as recursion, procedures and variables. The potential of Logo programming to become the basis for learning mathematics as envisaged by Papert (1980) and his colleagues has not been realized. However, Logo research has made an enormous contribution to our knowledge about the role which ICT environments can play in students' learning of mathematics.

ICT and learning mathematics

Nowadays there is a wide range of excellent computer-based environments available for learning mathematics. These include dynamic geometry environments, graph-plotting packages, statistics and data-handling packages and computer algebra packages. Spreadsheets, which were not developed for learning mathematics, are increasingly used both to introduce students to a range of mathematical ideas, and as a more general mathematical modelling tool. Interestingly our research on young people's use of computers at home shows that some young people are beginning to play around with spreadsheets at home. This seems to be because spreadsheets are viewed by young people as a professional tool for use within the adult world. Using spreadsheets could be considered to be a mathematical literacy practice which is a 'fund of knowledge' that moves between the school and the home.

However, despite the early advent of the use of computers for learning mathematics, despite the wide range of excellent computer environments now available for learning mathematics, despite the substantial research on teaching and learning mathematics with ICT, there is evidence that mathematics teachers are less likely than other teachers to capitalize on the potential of ICT for learning mathematics (Triggs et al. 2003). There are many possible reasons why mathematics teachers are reluctant to integrate ICT into their classroom practices.

First many of the computer-based environments such as dynamic geometry, computer algebra and spreadsheets are rich and complex environments. It is for this very reason that they are potentially productive technologies for learning mathematics. However, this also means that teachers have to learn themselves how to use these tools for doing mathematics.

Second, many of these mathematical tools are so powerful, have so much potential, that it is difficult for teachers to know where to get started. Dynamic geometry, for example, could be used to teach transformation geometry, it could be used to teach properties of circles, it could be used to teach functions and graphs. Although there are many books, articles and websites which provide ideas for getting started, ideas alone are not sufficient. Teachers need support in order to take the risk of beginning to use ICT in the classroom, especially when they are working within high-stakes assessment systems. Creating a support network for mathematics teachers was a central aspect of the InterActive Education project,[7] and the characteristics of such a network are discussed more fully in Chapter 7.

However, I believe that there is an inevitability about the eventual integration of ICT into mathematics lessons. Young people are increasingly using ICT at home for leisure, pleasure and work-related activities and they expect to use it at school. Even so, young people are discerning about its use and can distinguish between powerful new tools and superficial environments.[8] Within the rest of this chapter I present two examples of how ICT could be integrated into mathematics classrooms, the first relates to work in secondary schools and the second to work in primary schools.

Algebra and spreadsheets in the secondary school

In schools spreadsheets have been creatively used to develop activities for learning mathematics, even though they were not designed for this purpose.[9] Interestingly one aspect of a designed tool is that it will inevitably be used in ways which were not anticipated by the designer. Spreadsheets are part of the culture of many workplaces and in this sense are becoming part of everyday culture. Whereas the early spreadsheet was difficult to use, the spreadsheet interface has evolved considerably over the years and has become reasonably accessible to both primary and secondary school students.

In Chapter 3 I introduced the case of Eloise who at the age of 15 was already classified as low attaining in mathematics. Eloise was one of a whole class of low-attaining students who took part in a project which involved using spreadsheets to learn algebra.[10] The approach which was used with Eloise's class is what Teresa Rojano and I have called a spreadsheet-algebra approach (Sutherland and Rojano 1993). For Eloise this meant presenting her with the use of algebraic symbols within the context of a range of mathematical problems over a period of 4 months. Through this work with spreadsheets Eloise began to construct new meanings for 'letters as symbols'. She began to use 'spreadsheet symbols' to solve mathematical problems when working within a spreadsheet environment. She also seemed to be 'thinking with symbols' when solving problems on paper.

Eloise worked conscientiously on the spreadsheet activities with her partner Donna. They always wrote down the spreadsheet rules on paper (for example, for the square numbers they wrote down 'times the number by itself'). She was clearly motivated by this work as indicated by the following conversation which took place in an interview:

Int: Why do you think you have learned from using the spreadsheet?

Eloise: Because you've done different things and you've asked questions in a different way so you really think about what you are doing.

Int: Some people say that if you learn it on the computer you can only do it on the computer. Why is it that you can do it now when you are on paper?

Eloise: Because you have to think before you type into the computer anyway. So it's just like thinking with your brain. You think of columns.

Int: Is computer work too easy sometimes?

Eloise: No, computer work makes you think about what you are doing.

Int: How do you know you are thinking?

Eloise: Because your brain hurts ... don't know ... you really have to think about it before you put it on the computer or you just muck up all the spreadsheet.

The students in Eloise's class were asked to solve a range of word problems using a spreadsheet. At first they usually attempted to solve such problems using an 'arithmetic approach'. So, for example, when first using a spreadsheet to express a general rule for the perimeter of a rectangle Eloise typed in a rule using specific values (47*2 + 10*2). This drew on her knowledge of arithmetic and is how most students would start to solve such a problem. However, after an intervention from the teacher Eloise changed this specific rule to a general rule, by using a mouse to refer to the spreadsheet cells (two multiplied by the 'length cell' plus two multiplied by the 'width cell'). The use of the mouse seems to enable students to move in an effortless way from the specific to the general. When discussing her spreadsheet work with her partner Eloise started to use the spreadsheet code in her talk:

Eloise: Equals now what do you click on Donna ... so what will it be ... B2 times 2.

Although she always entered spreadsheet rules by pointing to the cell with a mouse she began to learn the spreadsheet code which was being entered into the computer (through seeing and saying). She also began to learn that the spreadsheet code represented any number.

After approximately 7 hours of spreadsheet work Eloise had learned how to use general rules and express these in both spreadsheet and algebraic code. When asked what she had learned from work with spreadsheets she said, *'Formulas . . . it's easier to work it out on the computer'*. At the end of the study Eloise showed how much she had been influenced by her spreadsheet work when answering the 'Chocolates Problem' (Figure 6.1) on paper away from the computer.

Chocolates Problem

100 chocolates were distributed between three groups of children. The second group received 4 times the chocolates given to the first group. The third group received 10 chocolates more than the second group. How many chocolates did the first, the second and the third group receive?

Figure 6.1 The chocolates word problem

Eloise's solution (with no computer present) illustrates the way in which the spreadsheet code was beginning to play a role in her thinking processes (Figure 6.2).

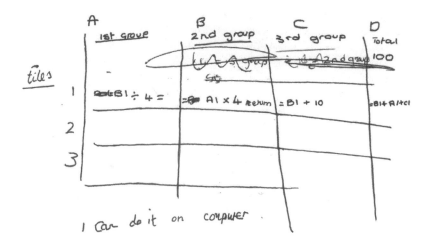

Figure 6.2 Eloise's response (on paper) to the chocolates problem

Eloise had drawn a spreadsheet on paper to support her solution and had correctly written down all the rules represented in the problem. She had not specified the unknown and if she had been working at the computer the 'circular reference' error message would have provided feedback on this error. When interviewing Eloise I asked her, 'if we call this cell X what could you write down for the number of chocolates in the other groups?'. Her first response was: 'so you're not doing add column' which supports the view that she thinks in terms of spreadsheet columns. I said, 'think of it as algebra' and she immediately wrote down:

$$= X \qquad = X \times 4 \qquad = X \times 4 + 10$$

When asked what she thought the X was she said, 'it can be anything' and she went on to say, 'X is a column, a place where you can work these out if you do something you couldn't work out you would just go onto the computer and type in different columns'. Eloise who had always been unsuccessful with school mathematics, had learned to use symbolic code to represent mathematical relationships. The spreadsheet symbolism had taken on a mediating role in her thinking of the unknown.

There was also a qualitative change in her response to other questions. In response to a question about the perimeter of a rectangle (Figure 6.3) Eloise

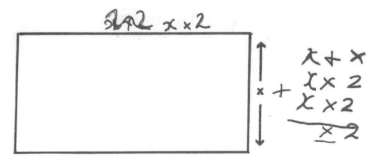

Figure 6.3   Eloise's response to the rectangle question in the post interview

was able to write down $X \times 2$ for the length without any support from the interviewer. When asked to write down the length of the perimeter she first replied, 'you really have to know what the numbers are don't you' showing that students cannot easily think in terms of something which is 'not yet known'. At this point the following interchange took place:

Int: You can't do it if you don't know what the numbers are?
Eloise: I suppose you could but I can't.
Int: Try and write something down.
Eloise: X times 2 times 2 again or you could do X times 2 and add them then times by 2.

Int:	This is X.
Eloise:	X plus X and then again.
Int:	Right now why do you think you found that difficult?
Eloise:	Don't know, I'm getting it mixed up with area.

After this exchange Eloise wrote down the sum which expressed the perimeter of the rectangle (see Figure 6.3).

In this example spreadsheets were being used as a tool to introduce Eloise (and her classmates) to the world of algebraic symbols. Eloise was beginning to develop an important aspect of symbol sense, namely friendliness with symbols.[11] There are many other approaches to introducing students to algebra as illustrated by the work of Alf Coles in Chapter 5. In all of these approaches students are learning to use symbolic tools to solve mathematical problems. In this sense symbolic algebra is transforming what they see and do; it is becoming a powerful new tool to think with.

Algebra and spreadsheets in the primary school

We also know from our research that primary students can work with spreadsheets to support them to learn algebraic ideas. Not surprisingly when they are first introduced to a spreadsheet they tend to attempt to solve problems using what could be called an arithmetic approach, which involves using specific numbers to solve a problem. The following example from 10-year-old students, Andrew and Graeme, is taken from collaborative work with Teresa Rojano (Sutherland and Rojano 1993).

Andrew and Graeme had been asked to use a spreadsheet to find expressions equivalent to 'multiply an unknown number by 4' (see Figure 6.4 for a similar activity). They entered the number 3 in cell A2 and then in another cell entered the formula A2*0.5*8, which produced a value of 12. In a new cell they then entered the expression A2*3 + 3 which they had worked out as being equivalent to 'multiply an unknown number by 4' because it also produced a value of 12. The second expression suggests that they were thinking with the specific number 3, and focusing on the process of calculation in order to construct the equivalent expression. When they varied the number in cell A2 they realized for themselves that two formulae were not equivalent and changed the second expression without any need for intervention from the teacher. Through this interaction with the spreadsheet they began to construct equivalent expressions of the form A2*2*2, A2*16/4, A2*32/8. In this example the feedback from the computer was sufficient to provoke them to reconsider their first constructions.

In this example the students moved from a focus on the process of calculating the value of the function X × 0.5 × 8 when the number 3 was input,

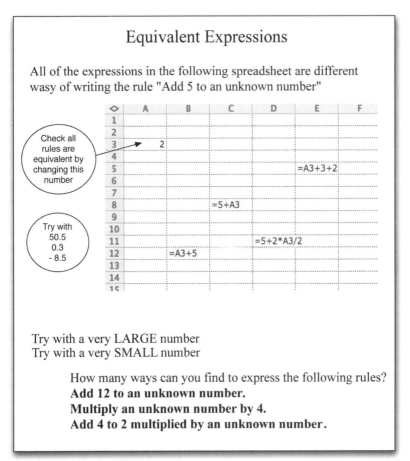

Equivalent Expressions

All of the expressions in the following spreadsheet are different wasy of writing the rule "Add 5 to an unknown number"

Check all rules are equivalent by changing this number

Try with
50.5
0.3
- 8.5

Try with a very LARGE number
Try with a very SMALL number

How many ways can you find to express the following rules?
Add 12 to an unknown number.
Multiply an unknown number by 4.
Add 4 to 2 multiplied by an unknown number.

Figure 6.4   Equivalent expressions in a spreadsheet

to a consideration of the relationship between such functions as X × 0.5 × 8 and X × 2 × 2 and X × 16/4. This type of activity could be extended by asking students to consider why the following types of statements are true:

$$3x + 7 = 2x + x + 7$$
$$5m + 4 + 3 = 3m + 2m + 7$$

This is a way into manipulating algebraic expressions, a way into mathematical proof, with the experimental work at the computer providing a basis for making conjectures about such statements (for further discussion of mathematical proof see Chapter 8).

As Teresa Rojano and I reported in 1993, the most important conclusion from this work is that spreadsheets can be used to support students to explore, express and formalize their informal ideas:

> I think that it helps you because you put what you think in and then you can check to see if you are right and it gives you more encouragement to continue because you know that even if you do it wrong you can use the spreadsheet to help you.
>
> (quote from a 10-year-old student, Rojano and Sutherland 1993: 380)

However, as we described in detail in the 1993 paper, the shift from an arithmetic to a more algebraic approach to solving problems was always accompanied by interventions from a teacher, nudging students from their spontaneous arithmetic approaches to the more algebraic approach, which involved thinking with unknown numbers. Respect is shown for the students' initial approaches and the teacher draws on these approaches when introducing students to new and algebraic approaches to solving problems.

Concluding remarks

Digital technologies for learning mathematics have evolved considerably since the early computer programs. New digital tools are easier to learn than computer programming languages and have more potential for integration into school mathematics practices. These technologies include software that has been predominantly developed for learning mathematics (for example Autograph[12] and dynamic geometry[13]), software which has been predominantly developed for mathematicians (for example Maple[14]), software of a mathematical nature which has been developed for the world of work (for example the spreadsheet Excel), and non-mathematical software that has been developed as a communication and a presentational tool (for example PowerPoint, wordprocessor). It also includes digital tools such as the interactive whiteboard.

What the examples presented in this chapter illustrate is that it is the inextricable relationship between person and technology that leads to the transformation of mathematical learning. Learning to use spreadsheets enabled students like Eloise to develop new symbolic tools for solving mathematical problems. These symbolic tools became internalized to the extent that they could be drawn upon later in paper-and-pencil situations. Through engaging in designed activities and through the intervention of the teacher these students also learned to shift from using spreadsheet symbolism to using algebraic symbolism. Algebraic symbolism could then become a new tool which offered new potentialities for solving mathematical problems.

Understanding the potentialities of different tools for different purposes is an important aspect of becoming a resourceful student, an important aspect of becoming a resourceful teacher. It is important to appreciate that whereas a spreadsheet may be an appropriate tool for modelling and solving problems it is not an appropriate tool for solving algebraic equations. Here a computer algebra system or paper and pencil might be the most appropriate tools.

Notes

1. 'The calculating engines of English mathematician Charles Babbage (1791–1871) are among the most celebrated icons in the prehistory of computing. Babbage's Difference Engine No. 1 was the first successful automatic calculator and remains one of the finest examples of precision engineering of the time. Babbage is sometimes referred to as 'father of computing', from website of the Charles Babbage Institute, http://www.cbi.uqmn.edu/exhibits/cb.html.
2. See Sutherland (1994).
3. See Noss (1988).
4. Hoyles and Sutherland (1989). Logo Maths Project (1983–86) funded by the Leverhulme Trust.
5. See for example Sutherland (1992).
6. See for example Hoyles and Noss (1992).
7. www.interactiveeducation.ac.uk: Sutherland et al. (2004).
8. For further discussion of this see Facer et al. (2003).
9. Healy and Sutherland (1990a, 1990b), Sutherland (1993b), Sutherland and Rojano (1993) and Abramovich and Nabors (1997).
10. The Mexican/British Spreadsheet Algebra Project; Sutherland and Rojano (1993).
11. For further discussion of symbol sense see Arcavi (1994, 2005).
12. A graph plotting software, http://www.autograph-math.com/. For a discussion of issues related to the use of graph-plotting software for learning mathematics see Goldenberg (1988).
13. For example Cabri Géometre (http://www.cabrilog) and Geometers SketchPad (http://www.keypress.com/sketchpad/). For a discussion on how this software can be used in the classroom see Laborde (1993, 2001), Healy and Hoyles (2001) and Goldenberg and Cuoco (1998).
14. Maple is a program designed to help you to plot graphs and do computations, both numeric and symbolic. See www.math.utah.edu/lab/ms/maple/maple.html.

7 Designing for Learning

> Inventors work with simple forms and objects that they know very
> well. Inventions do not emerge from elaborate processes but from
> ongoing involvements with familiar objects and simple practices of
> interruption, juxtaposition and resymbolisation.
>
> (Davis et al. 2000: 196)

Opening remarks

The word 'design' carries with it notions of producing, expanding and iter-
ating which are valuable in thinking about developing new ways of teaching
and learning. The idea of teachers as designers emphasizes the creative aspects
of teaching, emphasizes the idea of making choices – made with awareness of
freedoms and constraints.

Design is central to professions such as engineering and architecture.
Here design decisions are made in the moment, theory is mostly in the
background and is only brought to the foreground when the designer is made
aware of an intractable problem. This could be called evidence-informed
practice. It is different from the evidence-based practice of medicine in which
practitioners are often expected to consult the evidence before making a
decision; here theory is expected to be in the foreground. Teaching is more
like the practices of architecture and engineering than the practice of medicine. Teaching could be viewed as an evidence-informed practice, with theory
in the background and acting in the moment in the foreground. But teaching
is also different from architecture and engineering. Engineers and architects
design material objects and technologies which are mediated by social contexts. Teachers, on the other hand, design social contexts, which are mediated by material objects and technologies. Interestingly engineers and
architects do not always pay enough attention to the social contexts within
which their buildings and technologies will function and teachers do not
always pay enough attention to the technologies which could mediate the
social context of teaching and learning.

Conceptualizing teaching as a design practice is not a new idea. For many
years Brousseau and colleagues in France have developed the idea of 'didactical engineering' as both a research methodology and as an approach to
designing for the classroom. Didactical engineering centres around the idea of
designing mathematical problem situations which make it likely that

students will engage with the mathematical ideas which are at stake. Another key aspect of didactical engineering is the idea that the responsibility for solving the mathematical problems will be devolved to the students, managed by the teacher. The design process 'anticipates students possible strategies and the feedback these will introduce from the medium, and ensure that the mathematical knowledge aimed at by the situation can reasonably appear, at least as a collective form of knowledge, in the adaption process' (Artigue 2001: 112).

Ann Brown (1992) in the USA developed the idea of classroom 'design experiments' as a reaction to the more traditional psychological experiments. The focus of a design experiment was the complexity and mess of the normal classroom:

> The major problem of trying to conduct design experiments consisting of many interwoven aspects. Components are rarely isolatable, the whole really is more than the sum of its parts. The learning effects are not even simple interactions, but highly interdependent outcomes of complex social and cognitive interventions.[1]
>
> (p. 166)

The idea of designing learning activities is also central to the work of the neo-Vygotskists. For example Davydov (1991) and his team have developed a learning initiative for number and multiplication in the primary school. This design work bears some similarities to the work of the French school in that it pays considerable attention to a-priori analysis of concepts and their development in history. It also differs from the French idea of didactical engineering in that it pays considerable attention to the mediation of mathematical activity with technologies. In this respect Davidov's work is situated within a socio-cultural theoretical perspective and draws directly from the work of Vygotsky.

Artigue (2001: 112) has pointed out that 'globally there is no doubt that the impact of research, engineering work based on research, or even innovative work, on the reality of ordinary teaching practices remains very limited. Research has certainly partial responsibility for this phenomenon. In the past it has not paid enough attention to the conditions of viability of the engineering designs it produced . . .'. I suggest that one of the major reasons why 'research engineering work' has had little impact on teaching practices, is that the design work has not been carried out in partnership with teachers.

Within much of the design research discussed earlier there is an implicit attempt to find, through the process of design experiments, a universal approach to teaching and learning mathematical concepts, this could be called grand design with a 'capital D'. The focus of this chapter is on local design, or what could be called 'design with a small d'. This foregrounds the work of the teacher as designer of mathematical activities, whilst situating the teacher as part of a community of teachers and researchers.

Teachers as designers

As a mathematics teacher in 1982 I designed a new course in Logo programming for a group of 16–18-year-old students. This involved thinking about what I wanted students to learn, about starting-point activities and about how I would interact with students in the classroom. At the time my reflections on this course were: 'One of the most exciting aspects of the course for me was to watch a mixed ability group of students all absorbed by projects chosen by themselves to suit their own ability' (Sutherland 1984: 30).[2]

As a mathematics education researcher my work has always involved designing for learning with a particular focus on the use of digital technologies. In the early projects, for example the Logo Maths Project (Hoyles and Sutherland 1989), the researchers took the major initiative in the design process, in thinking about how to present Logo activities to students. I now view this way of working, although possibly important during the early stages of an innovation, as being inadequate for sustaining an innovation. This may be one of the reasons why mathematics teachers are not harnessing the potential of research on the use of digital technologies for learning mathematics, even though much of it has been published in journals for teachers.[3] In a later project, the Microworlds Project,[4] teachers were expected to design 'microworlds for learning'. However, this approach was also problematic as the teachers, although supported by a 30-day in-service course, were more or less expected to design these microworlds on their own. They found this difficult and were much less innovative than the project team had anticipated:

> The casting of the teachers as curriculum developers is problematic within the time limitations of an in-service course. Achieving a satisfactory product requires a vastly different range of skills of production and sequencing than is normally required of teaches to carry out their work in the classroom.
>
> (Sutherland et al. 1991: 29)

As researchers we had not recognized the importance of our role in supporting teachers in the design process. Interestingly at this time we also had not adequately recognized the importance of the teacher's role in supporting students in the classroom. Overall we were attributing too much importance to the computer-based tools which we were using. This is interesting because nowadays one of my biggest concerns about the use of digital tools in the classroom is that teachers devolve too much responsibility to the tools, not placing enough emphasis on their own role in the classroom.

This early work has evolved into a more productive way of working, in which teachers, researchers and teacher educators work in a collaborative team and each teacher, although responsible for designing for learning mathematics, is supported by the work of the whole team. This way of working was a key aspect of the InterActive Education Project,[5] and Simon Mills (Chapter 4), Rachel Zewde (Chapter 5), Marnie Weeden (Chapter 8) and Pat Peel (Chapter 8) were all partners in this project. The use of digital video has become an important part of this collaborative work, a central part of reflecting on and evaluating the teaching and learning process.[6]

This new approach to designing for learning has emanated from work at Bristol University. This is particularly apt as one of the greatest designers of the nineteenth century, Isambard Kingdom Brunel, developed one of his most famous designs in Bristol – the Bristol Suspension Bridge.

Interestingly Brunel's mother was English and his father was French, and so possibly Brunel's designs were influenced by both the more analytical French approach to engineering and the more pragmatic and creative British approach.[7] Just over 100 years later Concorde was designed in Bristol, again a collaboration between French and British engineers. I emphasize this Franco-British collaboration because it symbolizes what is possible when groups of people with different perspectives work together within a design process (see Figure 7.1).

Figure 7.1   Concorde's last voyage – flying over the Bristol suspension bridge

Design initiatives for mathematics

In some senses design is part of any innovation in the classroom, in that decisions have to be made about which mathematical activities and technologies are to be used. An important aspect of this design process is an imagining of how students will engage with the activities being proposed. This type of thinking ahead could be what Davis and colleagues (2000) call 'a thought experiment' in that it places emphasis on thinking through what might happen when the innovation is realized in the classroom.[8] Such a thought experiment has to consider the ways in which the particular students who are to be taught are likely to engage with the designed activities. This involves imagining how these students are likely to solve the problems to be presented, which also involves imagining the multiple histories of learning they are likely to bring to the learning activities. There are, however, risks associated with teachers placing too much emphasis on a-priori analysis and pre-planning as this could lead to attempting to follow pre-plans in a more or less rigid manner in the classroom. Another possible problem associated with pre-planning is that teachers could think that with adequate pre-planning they could then determine what students will learn. But this is not the case: 'the path of learning can never be determined by the teacher. However the path of learning is dependent on the teacher – along with a host of other contingencies' (Davis et al. 2000: 67).

This is an important point because it highlights the crucial role of the teacher, emphasizing that what the teacher does in the classroom will influence what students learn, but that teachers can never predict in advance what students will learn from any pre-planned learning activity. In this sense the mathematics classroom can be thought of as a complex dynamic system, which can only be modelled through running an iterative dynamic model of the system, and in which small changes in what a teacher or student says or does can lead to large changes in learning outcomes:

> Classrooms are complex systems. They exceed their components. They are more spontaneous – that is, alive – than complicated systems. Unlike complicated (mechanical) systems, which are constructed with particular purposes in minds, complex systems are self-organising, self-maintaining, dynamic and adaptive. In brief, whereas complicated systems tend to be framed in the language of classical physics, complex systems draw more on biology.
>
> (p. 55)

Developing ways of working in the classroom which are contingent on feedback from students is an important aspect of the overall design process.

This could be called building contingency into the design, where the use of the word contingency relates to the idea of 'circumstances that are presently unknown'.

This idea of design emphasizes both the idea of a 'thought experiment' in advance of teaching and the idea of teaching in the moment which will always be contingent on what happens in interaction with students when the design is realized in the classroom. From this perspective imagining and thinking in advance through situations should not constrain teaching and learning in pre-determined ways. Imagining and thinking in advance should enable a teacher to become open to all the possible learning trajectories. This approach to design, which evolved throughout the InterActive Education Project is characterized by five interrelated aspects:

1   partnership between teachers and researchers
2   research-informed practice
3   out of the classroom – design as a thought experiment
4   in the classroom – teaching in the moment
5   out of the classroom – reflection, evaluation and redesign.

In the following sections of this chapter I draw on the work of the InterActive Education Project to illustrate these five aspects of the design process.

Partnership between teachers and researchers

> Professional development requires a 'breaking out' of set roles and relationships in which researchers are traditionally seen as knowledge generators and teachers knowledge translators or users.
>
> (John 2006)

One way of breaking out of set roles is to create a partnership between teachers and researchers in which all members of the team bring their experiences and expertise to working together. Within the InterActive Education Project this was operationalized at three levels: the macro, meso and micro levels. In the centre (the meso level) was the Mathematics Subject Design team, a team made up of teachers and researchers.[9] This team had a life which was sustained by both face-to-face meetings and communication at a distance. When the team came together the focus was on hands-on work with digital technologies, discussion and designing, with members of the team contributing their expertise, some of which was grounded in classroom practice and some of which related to research evidence. Within this meso community teacher–researcher pairs (the micro-level teams) worked together on the more detailed design process, bringing ideas back to the meso community for critical feedback. This involved finding relevant literature, designing activities and diagnostic assessment. Design was informed by theory, research-based evidence on the use of ICT for learning, teacher's craft knowledge, curriculum knowledge, policy and management constraints and possibilities and the research team's expertise. The focus was on iterative design and evaluation and initiatives were piloted before substantive evaluation.

The work of the meso-level and micro-level teams was sustained at a macro level by a core team of university researchers, teacher educators, teachers and research students who worked together to develop the theoretical and methodological coherence of the project. Many of the participants in the macro community also participated in the meso- and micro-level communities but the communities were separate in their overall purposes:

- the macro-level community was concerned explicitly with theory development
- the meso-level community was concerned with research-informed design with the focus being predominantly on tacit knowledge (informal knowledge often expressed in processes)
- the micro-level community was concerned with design and realization at the level of the classroom.

Within this framework there was an omni-directional knowledge exchange between the three layers of the community which

> challenges the linearity embedded in traditional models of professional knowledge dissemination and re-model the relationship between the intersecting communities of research and practice so that effective pedagogy can be understood, developed and sustained.
> (Triggs and John 2004: 427)

The aim was to move beyond the idea of reciprocity where roles are retained (the researcher being the active enquirer and the teacher the focus of the enquiry) to a position where both teachers and researchers bring distinctiveness and complementarity to the knowledge-building process. The following extracts from interviews with mathematics teachers in the Inter-Active Education Project illustrate this point:

> People from an academic focus tend to look at things with a theoretical background. Teachers are always concerned with the practical. But we should be looking at teaching and learning more than we are able. The university partners are all teachers but each of you has a different perspective. It's been enjoyable – the different ways of

working. It has made me think an awful lot ... I think it's on my mind all the time.

And that was really nice to just be able to bounce ideas off somebody else. Because I think you are quite isolated when you are a teacher, you are in the classroom on your own and you do your own things in a way, not that in-depth because people don't have time in school. And I really enjoyed that aspect of it. And just that you were coming up with lots of new things that I hadn't thought of. And as well I really felt that you gave me a lot of confidence in trying out different things and you were just like, 'Yeah go ahead and just do it'.

From this perspective, innovation becomes the process by which individuals and groups create and define mutual problems and then actively develop new knowledge to solve them.

Research-informed practice

At the outset, research findings were presented formally through 'raw' texts. This soon gave way to a more flexible approach based on appropriateness. At times this meant sharing a research finding orally though what Bassey (1999) terms 'sound bites'; at others it meant being more complex and explaining ideas through more detailed discussion around a particular piece of evidence that had been chosen by the researchers on the request of the team. Here more complex discussions led to open debates which often touched on methodology, theoretical perspectives and findings. Again, what was important were the ways in which research validated knowledge was not privileged but opened up to contestation alongside other forms of knowledge that were more recognisable to the practitioner. This iterative approach also allowed research evidence to influence teachers' thinking as the teams and individuals examined new ideas in the light of well-established practices.

(Sutherland et al. 2005)

Working within the meso-level team each teacher in the mathematics design team chose a mathematical area which was to become the focus of their design initiative. For example Marnie Weeden (2002) chose to work on geometry and proof with a class of 13–14-year-old students, Simon Mills (2004) chose to work on data handling with a group of 8–9-year-olds, Rob Beswetherick chose to work on quadratic functions with 12–13-year-olds (Godwin and Beswetherick 2003). Having made this choice a central aspect of the design process was a consideration of research which could inform both the design of activities and practices in the classroom. This included a consideration of more general theories of teaching and learning and also particular research which related to the mathematical area to be learned (for example proof, multiplication, algebra). The wealth of research on learning particular areas of mathematics is potentially overwhelming. For example, there is a whole website on the teaching and learning of mathematical proof,[10] there are extensive and often conflicting perspectives on teaching multiplication[11] and substantial research on learning algebra.[12] The theoretical perspective on teaching and learning foregrounded in the InterActive Project (and in this book) was socio-cultural theory, which focuses on the idea that all action is mediated by both people and technologies, and that this mediated action is both socially and culturally situated (for further discussion see Chapter 9). However, within this framework teachers were supported to find the particular aspects of theory which would be most useful in helping them design for and interrogate their practice. For example, as Simon Mills explains below he became particularly interested in the work of Neil Mercer (1995) as it supported him to begin to understand the ways in which language was being used in his classroom:

> As an MSc student at the University of Bristol, and stimulated by a previous ESRC Funded project, the InterActive Education Project I had become increasingly interested in the work of Neil Mercer (1995), particularly his idea that classroom talk can be viewed as the 'social mode of thinking' and the primary vehicle by which shared understanding is negotiated and developed within learning situations. This 'Thinking Together', or 'Reasoning Together' idea had become a key element in my thinking when 'designing' teaching and learning contexts in the numeracy hour. The interactive whiteboard, as an interface, alongside selected software environments had come to play a central role in facilitating, scaffolding, supporting and recording the outcomes of these classroom based mathematical conversations, developed within my interpretations of the National Numeracy Strategy objectives.[13]

Out of the classroom – design as a thought experiment

Design as a thought experiment involves unpacking the conceptual domain which relates to the intended learning, understanding its history, understanding conceptual difficulties and anticipating how students might engage in designed learning activities. This also involves considering structuring resources such as the curriculum and the assessment system.

To make this a manageable activity within the InterActive Project we focused on relatively small mathematical areas, which students normally found difficult to learn. Mathematics design initiatives were realized over a short period of time, bounding the innovation process and making the possibility of evaluation and redesign more likely.

When entering the design process the ideas of Available Design, Designing and the Redesigned developed by The New London Group (1996) are useful concepts. These concepts emphasize the idea that humans are both inheritors of patterns and conventions of meaning and at the same time active designers of meaning: 'semiotic activity is seen as a creative application and combination of conventions (resources-available designs), that in the process of Design, transforms at the same time it reproduces these conventions' (Fairclough 1989). From this perspective all designing starts with 'available designs' and in recognizing this 'the process of shaping emergent meaning involves re-presentation and recontextualisation. This is never simply a repetition of Available Designs. Every moment of meaning involves the transformation of the available resources of meaning' (The New London Group 1996: 75). This idea of design recognizes the iterative and creative nature of meaning making:

> The Redesigned may be variously creative or reproductive in relation to the resources for meaning making available in Available Designs. But it is neither a simple reproduction (as the myth of standards and transmission pedagogy would have us believe), not is it simply creative (as the myths of individual originality and personal voice would have us believe).
>
> (p. 76)

A design results from a subset of choices of the many possible choices which have been considered and of course the many possibilities which cannot be considered. From this perspective developing awareness of available structuring resources is an important aspect of the design process, an idea which was introduced in Chapter 2. Interestingly teachers often impose more constraints on a situation than the system is actually imposing on them. For example, mathematics teachers in the UK have to work within the framework of the National Numeracy Strategy.[13] This framework recommends that teachers organize a mathematics lesson around what has been called the three-part lesson:

1   oral work and mental calculation (5–10 minutes)
2   main teaching activity (30–40 minutes)
3   plenary (10–15 minutes).

Some teachers become constrained by this strategy, developing rather formulaic approaches to whole-class and individual work. Other teachers work more creatively within the framework as illustrated by the work of Simon Mills discussed in Chapter 4, adapting the particular strategy so as to follow a rhythm of whole-class and individual work which fits their own tacit understandings of student learning:

> I think because it actually allowed us to break down what it was that we were trying to achieve and it has given us a structured view of the kind of mathematical ideas and concepts that we need to teach children. You know … I mean I remember teaching place value, for example, but I didn't actually realize why I was teaching place value. … I think in the past primary school teachers … and if I was to take myself as an example … I've thrown everything I can at the kids and hope that something has stuck. But what this [numeracy strategy] has actually done is allow me to look at mathematics teaching and to break it down into smaller bits and to see what children actually need to do and need to achieve.
>
> (Simon Mills, first interview)

Awareness of possibilities and constraints leads to a consideration of structure. Davis et al. (2000: 49) point out that the word 'structure' is linked to the words 'strew' and 'construe': 'structure was first used to describe how things spread out or pile up in ways that can't be predetermined, but that aren't completely random either. More the organic form of the vernacular building'. I particularly like this focus on the vernacular because it relates to what is built 'outside of the academic tradition'. 'The distinguishing feature of traditional vernacular is that design and construction are often done simultaneously on site by the same people. At least some of those who eventually use the building are often involved in the construction or at least have direct input in it's form'.[14]

Designing for learning can be thought of as a sort of modelling process in which it is important to identify what cannot be varied, that is, the invariants (for example the curriculum, the assessment system) and what can be varied, that is, the variables (for example the starting point problem, the technology to be used, the formative assessment), what is known (for example the age of the students) and what is unknown (for example the students' previous experiences of learning, how students will respond in the classroom). The possibility of design and redesign should take away a concern to 'find the best design' and should support getting started with a good-enough design, which can be reviewed more extensively within the redesign process.

Having chosen a class and a mathematical conceptual area and having become aware of the available structuring resources, the question is how to get started with the design process. An important first step is to unpack the conceptual area. One approach is to use a concept map as a tool for representing this process. This unpacking of a conceptual area will relate to the teacher's understanding and view of the conceptual area, the specified curriculum, and views about students' learning. Within the InterActive Education Project we aimed to make these starting points available for discussion by all members of a subject design team, so that teachers could become aware of alternative perspectives, and in the process begin to problematize the mathematical area they intended to teach. In this respect the work we were carrying out within the subject design team was not dissimilar from the work we intended teachers to carry out in their own classrooms.

Having scoped out the broad mathematical conceptual area it was then possible to set out learning aims and begin to think about the types of problems, artefacts, technologies and representational systems that would be used. All of this work involved anticipating the ways in which the students would be likely to engage with such problems (for further discussion on this process see Chapter 8).

Finding 'available designs' can become the starting point for developing mathematical activities. There are many extensive resources which can be used as a starting-point.[15] For example, when Simon was searching for a problem to present to his class of 8–9-year-olds to introduce them to ideas of data handling he found a suggestion for a problem in the work of Janet Ainley (1996). This was the starting point of the design process, and when this was realized in the classroom it was inevitably transformed by the students and Simon's interaction with the problem.

When considering the types of problems to be presented to students many design decisions have to be made. Which symbols will be used? Should the problem be presented in a more open or closed way? Some teachers tend to use more open-ended problems (see, for example, the work of Alf Coles in Chapter 5). Other teachers tend to use more closed problems (see, for example, the work of Rachel Zewde in Chapter 5). The use of digital technology potentially changes the way in which mathematical problems are presented to students. For example, should non-linear functions be introduced at the same time as linear function? Should non-linear functions be introduced before linear functions? However, many teachers when first incorporating digital technology into their classroom practices will take as a starting point the problems they have always used to introduce a mathematical topic. These can then be modified as part of a redesign process.

Central to the planning of a mathematics design initiative is thinking about ways of providing feedback on student learning in a formative way throughout the learning process. Digital technologies add a new dimension to feedback because in many instances students can become aware of the appropriateness of their mathematical constructions from feedback from the computer. For example, if students are using a graph-plotting package to construct functions which are parallel to the function $y = 7x + 4$ they can see from feedback from the computer whether or not their constructed function is actually parallel to the specified function. Diagnostic assessment (Black and William 1998) is another way of providing feedback on student learning. This allows the teacher to develop understanding of students' mathematical learning and when students are focusing their attention on ideas which are not part of the intended learning. Interestingly the actual process of developing diagnostic assessment can become an important and integral aspect of unpacking a conceptual area (this will be discussed further in the examples presented in Chapter 8).

Into the classroom – teaching in the moment

> The key quality of lesson planning is that it should support a sense of the dynamic and complex possibilities that might arise.
>
> (Davis et al. 2000: 99)

The work of preparing for a mathematical design initiative cannot possibly anticipate the way in which the complex interrelated variables will pan out when the design is realized in the classroom. It is not possible to anticipate the ways in which students will respond to the prepared problems, the digital and non-digital tools and the teacher's questions. It is not possible to anticipate the ways in which students will interact with each other. It is not possible to anticipate the individual personal histories which each student brings to the classroom situation. This might seem like a policy maker's nightmare. But for the teacher it is a central part of the creative process of teaching, probably the very aspect of teaching which gives pleasure and purpose. It is also the very aspect of teaching which makes it very different from architecture, engineering and medicine.

In the classroom a design initiative will take on a life of its own. For example, when Simon Mills realized his design initiative in the classroom (Chapter 4) he entered the flow of teaching, acted in the moment, acted in ways which were contingent on the students' responses in the classroom. When some students discovered that it was possible to construct a spreadsheet in Excel in which the area of each segment of a pie chart was represented (on the screen) as a percentage Simon used this opportunity to introduce mathematical ideas related to proportion and fractions. This had not been pre-planned, although Simon's systematic thinking through of the conceptual domain before he entered into the flow of teaching is likely to have supported him in responding to students' unexpected mathematical ideas.

Reflection, evaluation and redesign

An emphasis on redesign is aimed at working against the tendency to value the new and discard the old but, more importantly than this, it places an emphasis on learning and professional development. Learning from the old becomes part of a systematic process, part of building a research and development community.

In the classroom when a teacher enters into the flow of activity, it is almost impossible to reflect on one's own actions. It is impossible to see what all the students are doing, hear what all the students are saying. This is why digital video is a valuable tool which enables classroom interaction to be recorded and viewed soon after the process of teaching and learning has taken place (Armstrong and Curran 2006).

Viewing the video recording becomes part of a process of reflection which is a starting point for the redesign process. The following is part of Simon Mill's reflections on his work with the interactive whiteboard:

> In engaging with the video data from my classroom, what constitutes interactivity seems to be a constantly changing feast, appearing messy and disorganized as we engage in a range of social interactions mediated by a host of tools, social, physical and cognitive, negotiating shared meaning as we engage with the social semiotic texts available ... but what is clear is that the whiteboard alone does not encourage this phenomenon.

Viewing the video data is also part of the work of the meso-level design team, part of the process of communicating classroom practice within the larger group. As Ellie Coombs, a member of the InterActive Project explained:

> What is going on in classrooms is being communicated and it does make the project look real, real pictures in real classrooms. Seeing it helps you to make sense out of it – it communicates across the Subject Design Initiatives and gives you real models that you know are more than just tips for teachers.

Whereas viewing the video data is a starting point for beginning to 'see' different things in the classroom, what is 'seen' relates to an individual's theories about teaching and learning. In this respect theories are inevitably a lens through which we 'see' and make sense of video data, and redesign will also involve a process of retheorizing.

Concluding remarks

The focus of this chapter has been on designing for learning, with an emphasis on the role of teachers as designers, working in a collaborative team – a subject design team – of teachers and researchers. The three overlapping levels of partnership (macro, meso, micro) are a key aspect of this approach, which transforms 'action research' into a new whole which focuses both on reflective practice and reflective research, with theory being recognized as a tool for seeing differently, a tool for both teachers and researchers to extend their respective and joint practices of teaching and research. In Chapter 8 these issues are taken up again as I describe and analyse the work of two teachers from the InterActive Education Project, Pat Peel and Marnie Weeden.

Notes

1. The work of Anne Brown on design experiments has recently been expanded by a group which call themselves the Design-based Collective. See Kelly (2003).
2. This quote from an article written by me in 1984 uses the phrase 'ability', a concept which I now view as problematic because of its association with something inherently fixed about a student.
3. See for example Micromaths www.atm.org.uk/journals/micromath/articles/.
4. See Hoyles et al. (1991).
5. www.interactiveeducation.ac.uk.
6. For further discussion of this see Armstrong et al. (2005).
7. For a valuable discussion of the role of design in engineering see Ferguson (1993).
8. For further discussion of the idea of a Subject Design Team see Triggs and John (2004).
9. Rob Beswetherick, Jan Bovill, Chris Carter, Ellie Coombs, Marie Gibbs, Steve Godwin, Phil Hamilton, Gary Handley, Leila King, Ross Martland, Simon Mills, Heidi Moulder, Pat Peel, Rosamund Sutherland, Marnie Weeden and Rachel Zewde
10. www.lettredelapreuve.it/.
11. See for example Schmitlau (2003).
12. See for example Mason and Sutherland (2002).
13. For information on the National Numeracy Strategy see http://www.standards.dfes.gov.uk/numeracy/.
14. This definition is taken from the web-based wikipedia http://en.wikipedia.org/wiki/Vernacular_architecture
15. See for example the resources produced by the Association of Teachers of Mathematics (http://www.atm.org.uk/resources/index.html).

8 Learning Geometry

Introductory remarks

> Geometry then may well be a figment of our visual system but it is a figment that corresponds to significant features of the outside world, hence its unreasonable effectiveness.
>
> (*Cohen and Stewart* (1994: 187)

The overall aim of this chapter is to exemplify the ideas introduced in Chapter 7 through focusing on the work of two teachers, Marnie Weeden and Pat Peel. Pat, an experienced teacher in an inner-city primary school, designed a learning initiative for 10–11-year-old students to learn about the geometry of quadrilaterals. Marnie, a recently qualified teacher in an inner-city secondary school, designed a learning initiative for 13–14-year-old students to learn about geometry and proof. Both Pat and Marnie were working within schools which were under considerable pressure to raise the level of achievement of their students.[1]

Partnership between teachers and researchers

Both Pat and Marnie worked within the mathematics design team of the InterActive Education Project[2] and this gave them support to take the risk of innovating with embedding ICT into teaching and learning mathematics:

> *Int*:   So why do you think you took the risks?
> *Marnie*:   Because I could, because I actually had an excuse to, without messing up. And also the time factor. It's very very hard with the curriculum to take any bits of time out . . . and risk them . . . but what it seemed to show me was that by hands on they learnt the subjects anyway.

From the outset the aim was for the mathematics design team to understand how technologies can be embedded into the process of teaching and learning mathematics. At the first meeting we worked with transformations using dynamic geometry software and at the end of this meeting each teacher agreed to undertake a 'mini-design' initiative and report on this at the next meeting. This emphasis on getting started in the classroom had been influenced by my experience of working with mathematics teachers on ways of integrating ICT into teaching and learning mathematics.[3] I had learned that almost all teachers are anxious about innovating with computers in the classroom, and that the best way forward is to get started with ICT and bring this experience back to the group for discussion. In this way the members of a team can begin to develop a common purpose.

Pat had specialized in mathematics when she had trained as a primary-school teacher in the 1960s: 'It's a sheer fluke that I got into maths. I went to maths because there weren't very many students at college doing maths and I actually liked the head of the maths department, he was a very persuasive charismatic person who was desperate to have maths teachers'. Marnie had trained to be a teacher as a relatively mature student. She joined the Inter-Active Education Project when she was in her first year of teaching. She had very little previous experience of using ICT within the mathematics class-room, although she used ICT extensively at home. Marnie had always enjoyed mathematics, although in her first career she was a research scientist:

> I quite enjoy Maths. I find it very interesting and I hope that comes across when I teach it. I get quite bouncy about the whole thing. Saying to them, you know, that's what you're going to move into later on when you do your A-Levels ... so just trying to give them a wider expanse on it.
>
> I wasn't sure how I'd feel about teaching, but I can honestly say that I get up in the morning and I don't dread going to work. I look forward to it. Some days more than others ... so, to me, that's all I wanted out of life – to have a job that I enjoyed.

Before the third meeting of the team all teachers had been asked to decide which group of students they planned to work with, which mathematical area they wanted to focus on, and which ICT environments they were thinking of using.

Pat decided to work on geometry and properties of quadrilaterals with her class of 10–11-year-old students. She particularly emphasized that she wanted her students (for many of whom English was a second language) to know the names of different geometrical shapes. Pat had no previous experience of working with ICT environments for learning mathematics and so decided to investigate the potential of a range of possible software and asked the mathematics design team to give feedback on the software she was review-ing.[4] Interestingly this helped to give the group a common purpose and ultimately led to Pat rejecting this software, because of its non-mathematical nature. After some experimentation with dynamic geometry it was decided to develop a quadrilateral microworld[5] for Pat to use in her classroom. This involved Pat, Federica Olivero and myself working together in afternoon and after-school sessions over a period of several weeks. Pat very much valued working in a team which included both primary- and secondary-school teachers:

> It was really stimulating. Really rewarding talking to secondary-school teachers. I was very much in awe of them to begin with. I felt being a primary-school teacher that (a) I wouldn't understand what they were talking about and (b) I wouldn't understand the maths that they were doing. I did understand what they were talking about and the maths, well, if it went over my head, it went over my head. It was just one of those things.

Marnie decided to work on geometry and proof with a group of 13–14-year-old students. She decided from the outset to use the dynamic geometry software Geometry Sketchpad as this had recently been acquired by her school. She learned to use this herself through experimenting at home with the portable computer which had been given to her by her school.

Structuring resources – the schools

Pat worked in an inner-city multicultural primary school, which was part of an Education Action Zone (EAZ), a government-funded initiative to boost educational standards in inner-city schools.[6] As part of this initiative the school had recently been equipped with a networked computer room and interactive whiteboard (Figure 8.1). When Pat joined the InterActive Education Project she said that her ultimate aim was to improve the numeracy standards in her school.

Marnie worked in an inner-city multicultural secondary school which had also recently received funding for ICT equipment and had invested this funding in sets of portable computers and classroom-based projectors which could be used by teachers in their own classrooms (Figure 8.2). In Marnie's school teachers were also given their own portable computers.

As already mentioned at the time of this project both schools were under considerable pressure to raise the results of students in their schools. This meant that both teachers were very concerned that their work within the InterActive Project would not detract from their need to raise the mathematical attainment of students in their classes. In this respect both Pat and Marnie were working in situations where it was not always easy to take the time to experiment with new ways of teaching and learning mathematics. However, despite this and with the support of the mathematics design team both teachers developed design initiatives which had a positive impact on their students' mathematical learning.[7]

Figure 8.1 Computer room in Pat Peel's primary school

Figure 8.2 Marnie Weeden's mathematics classroom

Structuring resources – the curriculum

Both teachers worked within the constraints of the English national curriculum. Pat used the specifications detailed in Box 8.1 from the Primary Numeracy Strategy[8] as a guiding framework for her design work.

Box 8.1 Key Stage 2 National Numeracy Strategy

As outcomes Year 6 students should, for example:
Name and begin to classify quadrilaterals; using criteria such as parallel sides, equal angles, equal sides, lines of symmetry.
Know properties such as:

- a parallelogram has its opposite sides equal and parallel
- a rhombus is a parallelogram with four equal sides
- a rectangle has four right angles and its opposite sides are equal
- a square is a rectangle with four equal sides
- a trapezium has one pair of opposite parallel sides
- a kite has two pairs of adjacent sides equal.

Begin to know properties such as:

- the diagonals of any square, rhombus or kite intersect at right angles
- the diagonals of any square, rectangle, rhombus or parallelogram bisect one another.

Similarly Marnie worked within what is called the Key Stage 3 Numeracy Strategy[9] and in her work was guided by the specifications shown in Box 8.2.

In particular Marnie returned again and again to the difference between a practical demonstration and a proof throughout her learning initiative. This is likely to have been influenced by the emphasis which was placed on this in the Numeracy Strategy documentation: 'Distinguish between a practical demonstration and a proof. For example, appreciate that the angle sum property of a triangle can be demonstrated practically by folding the corners of a triangular sheet of paper to a common point on the base and observing the result. A proof requires deductive argument, based on properties of angles and parallels, that is valid for all triangles' (Box 8.2).

Structuring resources – the students

Within the InterActive Education Project ideas from socio-cultural theory were threaded throughout the work of the meso and micro level groups.[10] This theoretical perspective emphasizes the fact that students actively construct knowledge drawing on what they already know and believe

Box 8.2 Key Stage 3 Numeracy Strategy

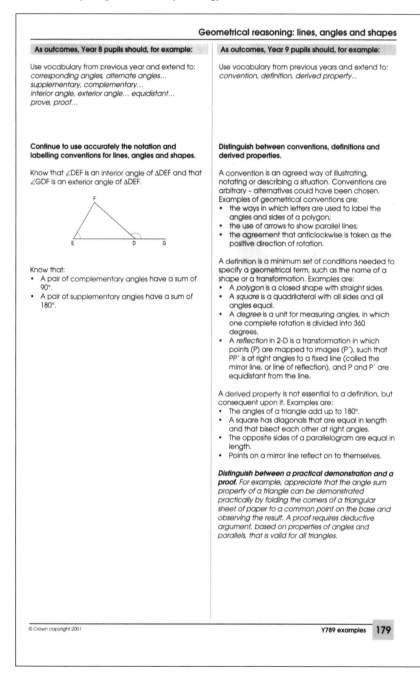

Geometrical reasoning: lines, angles and shapes

As outcomes, Year 8 pupils should, for example:	As outcomes, Year 9 pupils should, for example:
Use vocabulary from previous year and extend to: *corresponding angles, alternate angles... supplementary, complementary... interior angle, exterior angle... equidistant... prove, proof...*	Use vocabulary from previous years and extend to: *convention, definition, derived property...*

Continue to use accurately the notation and labelling conventions for lines, angles and shapes.

Know that ∠DEF is an interior angle of △DEF and that ∠GDF is an exterior angle of △DEF.

Know that:
• A pair of complementary angles have a sum of 90°.
• A pair of supplementary angles have a sum of 180°.

Distinguish between conventions, definitions and derived properties.

A convention is an agreed way of illustrating, notating or describing a situation. Conventions are arbitrary – alternatives could have been chosen. Examples of geometrical conventions are:
• the ways in which letters are used to label the angles and sides of a polygon;
• the use of arrows to show parallel lines;
• the agreement that anticlockwise is taken as the positive direction of rotation.

A definition is a minimum set of conditions needed to specify a geometrical term, such as the name of a shape or a transformation. Examples are:
• A *polygon* is a closed shape with straight sides.
• A *square* is a quadrilateral with all sides and all angles equal.
• A *degree* is a unit for measuring angles, in which one complete rotation is divided into 360 degrees.
• A *reflection* in 2-D is a transformation in which points (P) are mapped to images (P'), such that PP' is at right angles to a fixed line (called the mirror line, or line of reflection), and P and P' are equidistant from the line.

A derived property is not essential to a definition, but consequent upon it. Examples are:
• The angles of a triangle add up to 180°.
• A square has diagonals that are equal in length and that bisect each other at right angles.
• The opposite sides of a parallelogram are equal in length.
• Points on a mirror line reflect on to themselves.

Distinguish between a practical demonstration and a proof. *For example, appreciate that the angle sum property of a triangle can be demonstrated practically by folding the corners of a triangular sheet of paper to a common point on the base and observing the result. A proof requires deductive argument, based on properties of angles and parallels, that is valid for all triangles.*

(Vygotsky 1978). From this point of view students bring their implicit theories to any new learning situation and these influence what they pay attention to and thus new knowledge construction. In order to understand more about this perspective all students in both Pat and Marnie's classes were asked to carry out a diagnostic assessment before the subject design initiative started and six students from each class were interviewed.

The results of the assessment and interviews carried out with the students in Pat's class indicated that before engaging with the initiative they could name all of the special quadrilaterals apart from a trapezium. However, the majority did not know the properties of these geometrical figures. Some of the students interviewed said that parallel lines are like 'train tracks' which never cross (in response to a question about whether two lines which crossed were parallel one students said, 'no because if a train went along those tracks it would crash'). This image sometimes broke down with respect to the opposite sides of a rectangle. The longer pair of sides were said to be parallel but the shorter pair were said to be too far apart to be parallel. None of the students appeared to be able to make sense of perpendicularity and the majority of students could not identify an equilateral triangle from images of six triangles. For many of the students in Pat's class English was an additional language. Some of the students had very recently come to England as refugees and were learning English as well as learning mathematics. Pat was very aware of these language difficulties and this was one of the reasons why she initially wanted to focus on the role of language with respect to geometry.

The students in Marnie's class were in the top set of Year 9 (age 13–14). They were a bright group of students who had always been encouraged by Marnie to ask 'why' questions in the classroom. They knew about a range of geometrical properties but had never been taught about the ideas of mathematical proof. The results of the diagnostic assessment[11] carried out with the students in Marnie's class indicated that before engaging with the design initiative they knew very little about mathematical proof. When six students were asked in a pre-interview 'what is proof?' the majority of them gave responses which related either to everyday uses of the word, or to the idea of experiment:

> Is it kind of like a survey?
> Is it just like testing?
> When you get school photographs you get those little ones that say 'proof' on them. Is it like a sample or something?
> Show your workings.

However, one student's response showed a beginning understanding of the idea of proof:

> It's how to make sure ... to prove it, to say that is right because ...

Learning geometry – research-informed practice

As discussed in Chapter 7 one of the aims of the mathematics design team was to search for relevant research which related to the learning of the particular mathematical ideas that were the focus of each teacher's design initiative. The focus was on finding good-enough starting point articles to inform the design process and not on extensively reviewing the literature, although when available review articles were used. So for example a review article by Clements and Battista (1992) on geometry and spatial reasoning was particularly valuable in informing Pat's design. Analysis of the diagnostic assessment with respect to these concepts suggested that the majority of students in Pat's class were recognizing figures as visual gestalts, considered to be Level 1 of van Hiele's (1959/1985) levels:

> In identifying figures they often use visual prototypes. Students say that a given figure is a rectangle for instance, because 'it looks like a door'. They do not however, attend to geometric properties or to characteristic traits of the class of figures represented. That is, although figures are characterised by their properties, students at this level are not conscious of the properties.
>
> (Clements and Battista 1992: 427)

Articles and work by Zack and Reid (2000) and Olivero (2002) were valuable in informing Marnie's design. Research shows that the major difficulties of students' construction and understanding of proofs are represented by the coexistence of formal and intuitive aspects, which are manifested in the transitions from empirical to theoretical practices, from intuition to deduction (e.g. Balacheff 1988; Healy and Hoyles 2001; Olivero 2002).

The teachers within the design team brought their own interests and approaches to mathematics education research to the design process:

Marnie: When I was actually doing PGCE and we had to write those assignments for Laurinda[12] on maths. So I did quite a lot of reading about. I actually found him [John Mason][13] really interesting. And Alec had a lot of books in Cotham from when he'd been teaching PGCE. So I was really lucky to have an actual bookshelf just stacked with loads of stuff to look at.

Both Pat and Marnie chose to use dynamic software packages. The focus of learning in Pat's class was on the properties of geometrical shapes, the focus of learning in Marnie's class was on the interrelated aspects of properties, construction and proof. Federica Olivero's (2002) research on mathematical proof was very influential here, which had investigated the development of the proving process within a dynamic geometry environment:

> The representations of geometric objects in a dynamic geometry software are a way of bringing together formal and intuitive elements. GSP figures are midway between empirical and generic objects: they can be manipulated as empirical objects and the effect of this manipulation can be seen on the screen as it happens, but at the same time they incorporate geometric properties and as such represent generic mathematical objects.

Ideas from research were threaded through the design process, and in particular theory was viewed as a conceptual tool which could be used to see things differently in the classroom.

The first introduction to a new tool is likely to influence students' ongoing use of the tool and research has shown that students often start by drawing mathematical objects within a dynamic geometry environment as opposed to constructing objects from their properties. Marnie was aware of this literature and used the idea of the 'dragging test' (Healy and Hoyles 1994) from the beginning of her work with students:

> *Marnie*: Basically this is a session in which you become familiar with the software you are using . . . so I am going to show you first of all what the tools do, what you can do. But we are going to do some construction of a variety of shapes. But using what we know about those shapes. Using their properties.
>
> (Session 1)

Out of the classroom – design as a thought experiment

Pat's design

The design process involved working within the constraints of the situation in a creative and systematic way. For example, Pat wanted all her students to learn about quadrilaterals but within this constraint she considered:

- how to design a Cabri microworld which makes it likely that all students (whatever their confidence with language) will engage with both the properties of polygons and the names of these properties
- how Pat would work with the class in the computer suite and use the interactive whiteboard and other technologies
- what work students would do on paper and pencil in their normal classroom.

Throughout this process Pat was learning to use dynamic geometry through hands-on work on her home computer with support from the mathematics design team. The aims of Pat's design initiative were for 10–11-year-old students to learn:

1   to recognize particular polygons (quadrilaterals and triangles) and know the names of these figures
2   to characterize geometrical shapes by their properties
3   to classify figures hierarchically.

The decision to use a dynamic geometry environment was to enable students to manipulate for themselves, and 'see' mathematical properties, and the role of the teacher was initially to provoke students to become aware of what they were 'seeing' through spoken and written language. The dynamic geometry drop-down menus were customized for the purpose of this study, restricting them to: point, line, segment, circle, perpendicular line, parallel line, reflection, parallel and perpendicular (in the check property menu), distance and length, label, comments, colour, fill. This related to our view about the importance of structuring a learning environment so that students can creatively experiment within a pre-given structure.

Throughout the design process many decisions had to be made. For example, should students be presented with already constructed quadrilaterals, or should they be expected to construct quadrilaterals for themselves? Should students be presented from the beginning with all the 'special' quadrilaterals which they were expected to learn about, or should the starting point be asking them to focus on the similarities and differences between only two of these?

The focus of learning was on properties of quadrilaterals and we knew (from the diagnostic assessment) that students had very rough informal ideas about such properties. We decided that such rough ideas would not be an adequate starting point for them to construct quadrilaterals for themselves. The aim was for students to enter the world of mathematical properties so we decided that students should investigate these properties through playing with already constructed quadrilaterals. When students were more familiar with the properties of quadrilaterals we thought it would then be possible for them to construct properties for themselves.

The design initiative was planned to consist of six one-hour sessions as part of the primary-school numeracy hour. Only the first two sessions were planned in advance, the remaining sessions were developed in a more emergent way in the time between sessions. The following is an overview of each session:

*   Session 1 – playing with the quadrilateral microworld, introduce idea of properties

- Session 2 – noticing and writing about properties of quadrilaterals
- Session 3 – investigating diagonals of quadrilaterals (use the measure tool)
- Session 4 – investigating parallel and perpendicular lines
- Session 5 – playing with the triangle microworld and investigating properties of triangles
- Session 6 – black box game, three questions to guess which quadrilateral/triangle is in my box; students construct rectangle or parallelogram in Cabri.

Marnie's design

Marnie developed some rough ideas as a starting point for her design initiative (see for example Figure 8.3). From the beginning she was working on the difference between mathematical proof and demonstration (see Box 8.2) and this was a major emphasis throughout all of the sessions. There were several meetings between Marnie and the researchers (Federica Olivero and myself) and also ongoing communication by e-mail as illustrated by the message in Figure 8.4. This pre-planning (or thought experiment) enabled Marnie to problematize the mathematical area which was to be the focus of students' learning, although ultimately the sessions deviated in some respects from the pre-planning. What emerged was not always as had been planned as it was not always possible to book the laptops as indicated by the e-mail message in Figure 8.6.

Although Marnie had intended that the students would present their work on mathematical proof to the whole class, they initiated for themselves the idea of using PowerPoint as a proof presentational tool. This was likely to have been influenced by their use of PowerPoint in other lessons as they had not previously used PowerPoint in mathematics classes. As was the case with Pat the design of the sessions emerged over the whole period, with initial plans being modified in response to the ongoing work in the classroom. The following is an overview of the sessions of Marnie's design initiative:

- Session 1 – introducing dynamic geometry and the construction process
- Session 2 – proof or demonstration: identifying the difference
- Sessions 3 and 4 – proving that the sum of the angles in any triangle equal 180 degrees
- Session 5 and 6 – students presenting their proofs to the whole class (Weeden 2002).

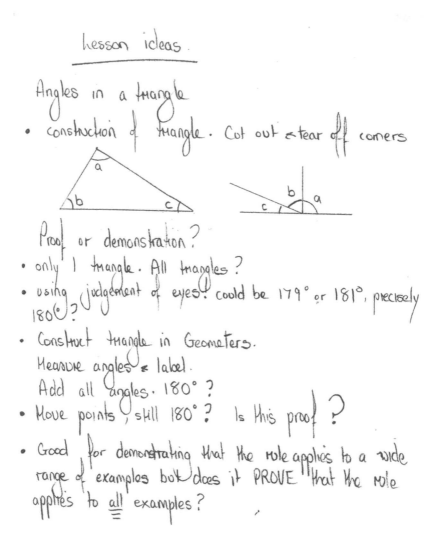

Lesson ideas.

Angles in a triangle
- construction of triangle. Cut out a tear off corners

Proof or demonstration?
- only 1 triangle. All triangles?
- using judgement of eyes! Could be 179° or 181°, precisely 180°?
- Construct triangle in Geometers.
Measure angles & label.
Add all angles. 180°?
- Move points, still 180°? Is this proof?

- Good for demonstrating that the rule applies to a wide range of examples but does it PROVE that the rule applies to all examples?

Figure 8.3 Marnie's draft planning

Into the classroom – learning about quadrilaterals

As mentioned earlier Pat realized that her design in the classroom was only partially influenced by the pre-planning, with many decisions being made in the moment as the design was being realized in the classroom. Within this section of the chapter I present an account of three of Pat's six sessions in order to illustrate the dynamic interactions between the teacher and the

Re: Re: Interactive Education   Tue, Jul 16, 2002 6:47 PM

From: <inter@stellar13.fsnet.co.uk>
To: "Rosamund Sutherland" <rosamund.sutherland@virgin.net>
Date: Sun, Mar 17, 2002, 8:37 AM
Subject: Re: Re: Interactive Education

Hi Ros

Just picked up your phonecall. Sorry I haven't been in touch but I came down with flu and didn't feel up to much. I have also had some problems booking the laptops due to a large demand for them. I haven't managed to book them for tomorrow as they were already booked for the whole day. I am finding that some days are like this! Tommorrow I will check all possibilities and book them, then we can decide which to keep.

On a positive side, I unexpectedly managed to obtain 10 laptops on Friday, last lesson, and some of the working groups that had done their HW and sussed out the proofs, were allowed to begin creating their presentations. I was highly impressed, some wonderful work has been going on (I'll send you 2 but Sssh! don't tell them that you've had a sneak preview!). Christine and Ashley came with theirs intact and just needed sketchpad to import, that's enthusiasm for you. They were so proud!

I've decided though that I'd still like to give them the opportunity to work on their project again with the laptops as I'd noticed that some groups had only just negotiated the proofs last lesson, and it would be a shame not to allow them the opportunity to join in with the fun.

On a darker note, I also noticed that several groups just seem lost without direction. These groups are, funnily enough, the groups that find it difficult to stay on task in general and appear to still not have a clue what on earth is going on. This also feels relevent to the work (ie. the lost souls of the project!!!)

I promise I'll contact you tomorrow as I feel a little more lively.

Marnie

Figure 8.4   E-mail message from Marnie Weeden – part of the evolving design process

students and the technology. The account is based on analysis of video data and also field notes.

Session 1 – playing with the quadrilateral microworld, introducing the idea of properties

The first session started with the teacher (Pat) working in the computer suite, with all students sitting as a class in the middle of the room paying attention to the interactive whiteboard (see Figure 8.1). On a flipchart at the front of the class (and to the left of the interactive whiteboard) Pat had written the words: Quadrilateral, Square, Rectangle, Parallelogram, Rhombus, Kite and Trapezium (these words were also on paper by each computer). Pat showed students (on the interactive whiteboard) how to move the quadrilaterals, how to colour in a quadrilateral and how to label it with its name, introducing this activity in the following way:

Pat: And we've got here set up for you on the computers . . . special
            new software . . . it's brand new to our school . . . it's been

brought in specially . . . it's been adapted and created for you . . . and here we've got a collection of quadrilaterals . . . 4-sided shapes . . . I'm going to show you how to use this . . . up here we've got a toolbar . . . most of that toolbar for the first task you don't need to know about . . . right, these shapes here you've got to know the names of them . . . does anyone know what that shape is called?

As Pat pointed to each particular quadrilateral she asked the students to name it and there was always at least one student who was able to do this. Pat then manipulated each quadrilateral on the interactive whiteboard, emphasizing that it always stays the same shape: 'it stays a kite all the time'. She then showed the students how to name each quadrilateral on the screen and finally said, '*Your task is to go to your computer and learn two things . . . learn . . . find out to move the shapes . . . how to move them around and to make them bigger . . . and the second task is to write the name of each shape by the side of it . . . has anyone got any questions?*'

Analysis of the video recording[14] shows that two of the students, Zacharias and Michael,[15] spent considerable time moving each individual quadrilateral and also filling them with colour. Although they did not talk extensively as they moved the quadrilaterals on the screen they used language such as:

What was that . . . oh yes a square . . . it doesn't look like a square now [as they moved the square].
How can we make it a square, that's a square . . . what was it . . . a rectangle . . . [as they moved the rectangle].
How do you make it bigger again?
You could just make it a line.
That looks like a clock [rotating the sides of a trapezium].
Let's make a bumper.
This is a boomerang.

Their spoken language gives an indication of where they were focusing their attention and the actions they were carrying out. They were beginning to notice, for example, that a rectangle can be transformed into a square. Sometimes their language referred to the world outside mathematics (for example 'this is a boomerang'), sometimes to the world of mathematics (for example 'it doesn't look like a square now again?') and sometimes to the process of transforming a shape (for example 'how do you make this bigger again?'). This shows how students draw on everything they know about in order to make sense of a situation. Zacharias and Michael did not name any of the quadrilaterals until the teacher explicitly intervened and told them to do this. By the end of the session they were able to name three of the quadrilaterals, which suggests that they had begun to identify these mathematical objects. Their spoken language, although not extensive, was focused on the task and appeared to support them in identifying the quadrilateral shapes.

Another pair, Chantale and Candice, approached the activity rather differently. They first filled in all the quadrilaterals with colour and then very systematically (and correctly) labelled each quadrilateral, paying considerable attention to spelling. It was only after this process that they then started to manipulate each quadrilateral saying things like:

> That looks like a kite now [as they moved the general quadrilateral].
> That looks like a parallelogram [as they moved the rhombus].
> Move the rectangle ... you click and pull, you click and pull.
> It's too skinny [as rectangle width is decreased].
> That looks like a parallelogram [as move kite].
> Do it tiny.
> Looks like a shoe [as trapezium is moved].
> I want it skinny.
> That's not a square ... it's a mouse head (as they make the square into a dot) that's too fat ... it's like train tracks [as they move the parallelogram].

Their spoken language suggests that they were mostly focused on relating the mathematical shapes to objects in the world outside mathematics (for example 'that's not a square, it's a mouse head'). The teacher did not intervene to suggest that these students shift their attention to the more mathematical aspects of the activity, probably because working with a whole class it is difficult for the teacher to engage with all the student groups.

Approximately 15 minutes before the end of this session Pat called the class back together for a final plenary session, saying:

> I was so impressed and so excited ... you did it much quicker and everyone in the whole class managed ... for what I could see nearly all of you were able to label them accurately ... I can see that all of you could label the shapes ... now can anyone tell me anything special ... any special properties ... any special things about a square ... any special qualities it has ... it always has...

This focus on the properties of quadrilaterals elicited the following types of responses:

- (for a square) – all sides the same length, it is a quadrilateral
- (for a rectangle) – not all the sides are equal, a four-sided shape, it's longer than a square

- (for a parallelogram) – they are diagonal, the sides are diagonal, the sides are like train tracks, there's two parallel lines on there
- (for a rhombus) – like a square, if you squash a square you get a rhombus, they are parallelish
- (for a trapezium) – like a triangle with its top off.

This plenary session was important in drawing the whole class's attention to the purpose of the work, namely to learn about mathematical properties of quadrilaterals.

Session 2 – noticing and writing about properties of quadrilaterals

Pat started this session by working with the whole class. She said:

> This is the second week of six weeks and our objective by the end of the six weeks ... you will be able to recognize shapes ... you will be able to name them and you will be able to tell me and other people some of the properties of those shapes ... how we can describe a shape ... what makes it different from other shapes?

Pat had written the names of the quadrilaterals on a flip chart and had made cardboard cut-outs of each quadrilateral. She picked one of these and asked a student to place this on the flip chart next to its name. As they did this she said:

Pat:	Can we all say that word?
All:	Trapezium.

This process was repeated for each quadrilateral. Pat then introduced them to what she called 'new mathematical vocabulary'. The following words had been written on the board (and were also on paper besides each computer): opposite, equal, parallel, adjacent, angle, sides, right, diagonal. Pat went through each word in turn explaining its meaning, sometimes bringing students up to the front of the class (for example to demonstrate opposite, and adjacent) and sometimes holding up pieces of card (for example to demonstrate parallel lines). However, as we shall see later, some of this activity seems to have caused students to become confused about the mathematical meaning of the words opposite and adjacent.

After this flip chart activity Pat moved to the interactive whiteboard saying:

| *Pat*: | Look at the screen ... we've got a rectangle and a parallelogram [Pat moves the shapes and emphasizes that all the time they |

stay the same shape] . . . now can somebody describe to me . . . let's look at the rectangle first . . . who can tell me anything about a rectangle which is special to it . . . Zacharias . . .

Zac:　　Opposite sides are the same size.

Pat then showed the students how they could write the properties of a quadrilateral on the screen. They then worked in pairs at the computer continuing with this activity (see for example, Figure 8.5).

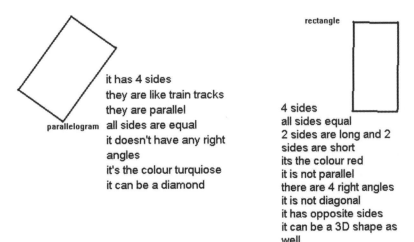

rectangle

it has 4 sides
they are like train tracks
they are parallel
parallelogram　all sides are equal
it doesn't have any right
angles
it's the colour turquiose
it can be a diamond

4 sides
all sides equal
2 sides are long and 2
sides are short
its the colour red
it is not parallel
there are 4 right angles
it is not diagonal
it has opposite sides
it can be a 3D shape as
well

WHAT IS THE SAME AND WHAT IS DIFFERENT?

Figure 8.5　Similarities and differences between a parallelogram and a rectangle: work produced by one pair of students in Session 2

Most students wrote something on the screen. For example for a parallelogram:

> Two parallel sides, opposite sides, four vertices, four right angles.
> It has four sides, they are like train tracks, they are parallel, all sides are equal, it doesn't have any right angles, it's the colour turquoise, it can be a diamond.
> The parallel opposite and it can be a square and a kite.

For a square:

> All sides are equal, four right angles, four vertices, opposite
> all four sides are equal, has four right angles, all sides are opposite.

For a rectangle:

> Four sides, all sides equal, two sides are long and two sides are short, it's the colour red, it is not parallel, there are four right angles, it is not diagonal, it has opposite sides, it can be a 3D shape as well.
> All sides are adjacent, opposite sides are equal, opposite sides are parallel, four vertices.

For a trapezium:

> Four vertices, three right angles, no equal sides.

For a kite:

> A kite has two lines the same length, it's got two diagonal lines.

Some phrases are difficult to make sense of, for example 'all sides are equal' for a parallelogram and a rectangle, but we think the students meant by this 'each side has a side which is equal to it'. Some phrases are non-mathematical (at least in this context), for example 'it's the colour turquoise' and some relate to transformations, for example 'it can be a diamond'.

Session 6 – black box game

At the beginning of this, the final session, Pat (T) introduced the class to a black box activity, in order to focus the students' attention on the properties of quadrilaterals:

> *T:*   I'm going to start off today with a game in my box here I have some shapes and you are going to guess what the shape is ... if you guess within five guesses a point you ... if you don't guess within five guesses ... a point to me ... now you will ask questions to which I can only answer yes or no ... the first three questions you can't say is it a square ... is it a triangle ... is it a rhombus ... is it an iscosceloes triangle ... you've got to ask questions thinking about the properties of the shape ... right ... for example ... let's begin ... I've got a shape here ... ask me questions about my shape ... you're allowed five questions and you keep a tally mark of the no of questions we've had ... a trial run ... next question ... Zacharias ...
> *A:*   Is it a quadrilateral?
> *T:*   Yes ... it is a quadrilateral.
> *T:*   Who'd like to ask the next question ... Emma ...

E: Has it got parallel sides?

T: Has it got parallel sides? Yes it has ... so you need to be thinking a shape that's got parallel sides ... a shape that's a quadrilateral and a shape that has not got three sides ... can you think of a question to do with the angles ... would you like to guess a shape now, Rasheen ...

P: A square.

T: It is a square ... the opposite sides are parallel ... it has got four sides ... they are all the same length and each angle is 90 degrees [T hold up square shape from box].

This activity which was carried out without computers showed that the students were developing an awareness of properties of quadrilaterals as illustrated by the following questions from the students:

Has it got an acute angle?
Is it an isosceles triangle?
Has it got any right angles?
Has it got equal sides?

Confusion related to the meaning of adjacent sides (which the analysis of data had shown was emerging in the second session) was evident in this final session, as the following interchange shows:

Emma: Has it got any adjacent sides?

Pat: Has it got adjacent sides ... they've all got adjacent sides ... all got sides next to each other.
And then later in the same session:

Emma: Are the sides adjacent?

Pat: All the sides are adjacent ... every shape we've got whether it is a triangle or a quadrilateral ... that side is adjacent to that one.

It seems that whatever meanings the students originally constructed for the word adjacent in Session 2, no amount of 'telling' by the teacher was impacting on these meanings. (The question in the post-initiative diagnostic assessment which asked, 'are adjacent sides equal?' for a range of shapes was answered incorrectly by the majority of students.)

After this activity Pat worked at the interactive whiteboard and showed students how to construct a rectangle for themselves. She then asked students to work in pairs and construct either a rectangle or a parallelogram. The students found this relatively difficult, but some of them, with support, were able to successfully construct quadrilaterals for themselves.

Reflections on Pat's design initiative

Analysing the processes of teaching and learning throughout this design initiative suggests that manipulating the geometrical shapes on the screen had helped the students to pay attention to similarities and differences between properties of different quadrilaterals. Analysis of the data suggests that students were learning:

- to use dynamic geometry as a tool for doing mathematics
- to become aware of mathematical properties of quadrilaterals and triangles and to talk about these properties
- to shift attention from extra-mathematical to intra-mathematical meaning
- to identify and name particular quadrilaterals.

The data also indicated that the way in which Pat orchestrated the session through talk and interaction with students was a key aspect of this work. For example, at the beginning and end of each session Pat directed the students to pay attention to the naming of quadrilaterals and the properties of quadrilaterals and she did this through her own use of language and through eliciting students' ideas.

Careful design of both the starting point activity presented by Pat and also the mathematical microworld developed in dynamic geometry seems to have been important in focusing students' attention on mathematical activity. Once students began to see the quadrilaterals on the screen, through the mathematical framework of properties of quadrilaterals, they were then able to say and write what they saw (as illustrated in Figure 8.5). This 'saying what they see' and 'writing what they say' also appears to have been important in terms of their mathematical learning. Writing on the screen appeared to be easier than writing on paper for the lower-attaining students. The students' writing also gave the teacher feedback on their developing conceptions, as did their discussions at the beginning and end of each session. The work with the interactive whiteboard allowed students to share and communicate their ideas and collectively focus their attention on properties of quadrilaterals. In this respect this collective work helped to make learning visible.

When students worked in pairs at the computer what they did was a creative imitation (see Chapter 9) of what they had observed Pat doing and what Pat had told them to do. However, because each student brought their own history of learning to any new learning situation each student constructed different meanings as they worked in pairs. Analysis of the data suggests that the seeds of the students' language could be found within Pat's language and gesture and what was written on student handouts. For example, the antecedents of the students' ongoing confusion related to the mathematical meaning of 'adjacent' could be found in the way this idea was introduced to students in Session 2. On one of the worksheets presented to students were the following questions:

- What have you found out about the sides of each shape?
- Are any sides the same length?
- Are they opposite sides?
- Are they adjacent sides?
- Are any sides parallel?

The words 'parallel' and 'equal length' relate to properties, but the words 'adjacent' and 'opposite' describe mathematical states. They are qualitatively different types of words and using all phrases together seems to have confused the students with respect to the mathematical meaning of adjacent and opposite.

The geometry design initiative was reworked and taught again to a new group of Year 6 students in the following year. From watching the video recordings Pat had become very aware of the subtle ways in which students transform language and activity for themselves actively constructing knowledge (for example 'like train tracks' for parallel lines becomes 'short sides of a rectangle cannot be parallel because they are too far apart'). In the revised design initiative, Pat planned to make more use of writing on the screen (see for example Figure 8.5) by printing out this work for students to annotate and comment on by hand within sessions in the normal classroom. In this respect the computer print-outs became resources for students to use for their ongoing learning and reflection. Pat also decided to make the revised design initiative more challenging for students: 'I think in the second one we upped the level of ability. I think we were more ... we thought these children can do more than this. Which is what they've been saying about lots of schools – teachers don't have the high expectations that they should have'.

Into the classroom – learning geometry and proof

Session 1 – construction and mathematical properties

Marnie started the first lesson by distributing the portable computers around the class:

- to become familiar with Geometers' Sketchpad
- to use this software to investigate construction using facts and properties of shape
- to investigate angle relationships involving parallel lines.

Marnie introduced students to the dynamic geometry software, drawing attention to the importance of using mathematical properties in the construction of mathematical objects. She said:

> What I want to point out to you ... all of you ... is that we have aims ... reasons we want to be here together ... things we want to get out of this session ... things we want to do ... basically this is a session in which you become familiar with the software you are using ... this is a program which I don't think any of you have used before ... so the aim of this is for me to kind of demonstrate to you the sorts of things you can do with this program or some of them ... because there are in fact loads ... this is a brilliant dynamic piece of software ... so I am going to show you first of all how to kind of use things, what the tools do, what you can do, what your possibilities are and we are going to do that initially by doing some construction. But we are going to do some construction of a variety of shapes. But using what we know about those shapes. Using their properties.

As Marnie demonstrated to the students how to use dynamic geometry to construct a square (through projecting her portable computer image on a screen at the front of the class) she explicitly modelled her own knowledge of construction processes, emphasizing that she was explicitly using the properties of a square and that *'there's always right angles in it and the construction remains the same ... just different sizes'*.

After this introductory phase the students worked in pairs on portable computers and tried for themselves to construct a square. Throughout this work as Marnie became aware that not all students were using mathematical properties she intervened again:

> OK we've had something interesting here. Someone has just found out ... they thought they were clever and drew a square, measured it, measured the angles, and guess what, it didn't stay. Moved it about and suddenly it was a quadrilateral of all sorts of different dimensions. It has to stay ... this one went all over the place because it wasn't constructed. You've got to use what you know are the properties and utilize them in this construction. Otherwise it will break ... just drawing lines will not work ... you need to actually use your knowledge of shapes in order to construct it. You need to use commands like the perpendicular bisectors, like parallel lines, that's what you need to do. Without actually using commands like that, using the constraints of a circle, circumscribing things, stuff that you know...

> (Session 1)

This focus on properties continued throughout the whole design initiative. In the third session when the students had been asked to construct a rectangle Marnie again focused on mathematical properties:

> And unlike the square you've got less constraints with that . . . so you know how to construct a pair of parallel lines . . . so you should be able to produce a proper rectangle . . . just to remind you because it's been a while . . . we didn't have the laptops last time.
>
> (Session 3)

A focus on mathematical properties, a crucial part of constructing mathematical objects within dynamic geometry, was also important when students began to construct their own mathematical proofs and was evident in the final proofs which students presented to the whole class (using PowerPoint) at the end of the learning initiative (see for example Figure 8.6).

Triangles on parallel lines

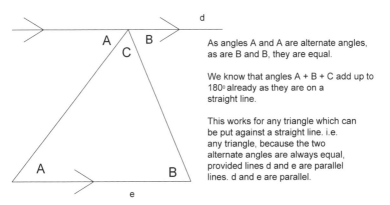

As angles A and A are alternate angles, as are B and B, they are equal.

We know that angles A + B + C add up to 180° already as they are on a straight line.

This works for any triangle which can be put against a straight line. i.e. any triangle, because the two alternate angles are always equal, provided lines d and e are parallel lines. d and e are parallel.

Figure 8.6   Excerpt from final PowerPoint proof for one group of students

Session 2 – the difference between proof and demonstration

Marnie started the second session by emphasizing the difference between proof and demonstration:

Marnie: If I say proof what do I mean?
Rob: Gathering evidence . . . in order to back . . .
Sarah: Exploration.

Marnie: Gathering evidence to support a theory, conjecture? ... In science we repeat an experiment loads of times. Is that mathematics proof as we know it? There is a difference between proof and demonstration ... are your eyes and the way your brain works enough for you?

Marnie then introduced a proof that the angles of a triangle add up to 180 degrees. She started by constructing a triangle in dynamic geometry, measuring the angles, finding they added up to 180 degrees and then asking if this was a proof. After soliciting a range of responses she again emphasized that measurement is not mathematical proof.

Within the third session students worked in pairs with dynamic geometry to develop their own mathematical proofs that the sum of the angles of any triangle is 180 degrees. Despite Marnie's discussion about what constitutes a mathematical proof the majority of students started to use the measurement tools to construct a proof. This is likely to relate to their previous experiences of measurement in geometry and the types of empirical proofs (Balacheff 1988) which they were likely to have been introduced to in primary and early secondary school. The following excerpt illustrates how Rachel and Jess started to explore the possibility of measuring:

Rachel: Is there some way we can calculate what J, K, L and M add up to?
Rachel: We'll just have look around [they start to look through the menus].
Jess: Oh ... angle bisector ... that looks fun.
Rachel: So I guess we'll have to highlight an angle.

By experimenting they discovered how to measure an angle. They then discovered the calculator tool and started to sum the angle measures. At this point Marnie, becoming aware of their activity, intervened to the whole class:

Before you go off on a tangent which is where you seem to be going ... you need construction but the other important thing is don't get het up and caught up in the measuring ... measuring is not proof ... you've already said that ... measuring is not proof ... for a start computers can make mistakes ... also for the particular computer program it tends to measure to the nearest point. Zero point something ... so what you'll end up with is something which doesn't equal 180 degrees ... when you've measured it will add up to 181. So you cannot rely on that software. And the reason we are here doing this now is proof ... so don't get muddled up with the measuring ... measuring is not proof ... it is being able to apply what we know about our angle laws to a situation in order to come out with some kind of reasoning, mathematical reasoning as to why that may add up to 180 and I know some of you are nearly there...

Interestingly Marnie had shown the students how to measure lengths and angles within Session 1, unwittingly drawing attention to the measurement tools. Although measurement cannot be used as a part of mathematical proof, it can be very useful in the phase of exploring, conjecturing and validating a conjecture within a dynamic geometry environment. The need for measures comes from the perceptual level when students have the intuition that, for example, two sides of a figure are equal, or one equals the double of the other and so on; however, when they read measures on the screen, or on paper, they are no longer working at a purely empirical level. As Olivero (2002) has suggested measures work as a tool which can provide an answer: yes/no. The quantitative side of the information linked to the use of measures makes students feel safe and certain about a result and can provide a solid starting point for the subsequent construction of a proof.

Analysis of the video data showed that Jess and Rachel eventually stopped measuring and started to construct proof statements on the screen:

Angles A, B, C and D are all right angles, they are 90 degrees and are all in rectangle so all the angles in the rectangles add up to 360 degrees. Angles j,k,l and m are an average of 45 degrees each.

Whereas these 'proof statements' could be criticized for being rather empirical and descriptive, they did provide a starting point in terms of supporting these students to enter the world of mathematical proof.

Sessions 3 and 4 – producing proofs

All the students produced their final proofs in PowerPoint and presented them to the whole class. An analysis of the final proof produced by Joanna, Rachel and Rick shows that they have moved from a focus on measurement to the production of a proof which contains logical justifications for what they observed on the figure.

All the students shifted from early uses of measurement to the construction of theoretical proofs and Marnie's ongoing interventions played an important role in this respect. These interventions were based on Marnie's observations of student activity in the class, her own a-priori analysis of what constitutes mathematical proof (see for example Figure 8.3) and her engagement with the research literature. Marnie created a collaborative classroom community which empowered the students to share their ideas and progressively refine their ideas about what constitutes a mathematical proof:

Marnie: Remember that there is no wrong or right here there are just ideas. There is just us coming together with ideas and that is us learning from each other about what we're doing and this is to do with working collaboratively together. OK, learning to work together and come together with our ideas.

(Session 1)

Reflections on Marnie's design initiative

Analysis of the data shows that throughout the learning initiative Marnie continued to emphasize the relationship between construction and mathematical properties and the difference between proof and demonstration. Whereas there is no simple relationship between this focusing of attention and students' activity, analysis of the whole design initiative showed that across the series of sessions there was a convergence between students' and teacher's perspectives. Students imported their geometrical diagrams from dynamic geometry into their PowerPoint proofs. The work with dynamic geometry is likely to have supported them to focus on the mathematical properties which became key aspects of their proofs:

Marnie: I asked them that as well. And that was exactly one of my questions. And what they said was that being able to move the things about enabled them to see things that if it were just a straight 2D stagnant drawing they wouldn't have been able to see at all.

All the students produced final proofs in PowerPoint and as a digital tool this seems to have offered considerable potential in terms of supporting students to focus on the importance of linking together a set of deductive statements to be presented to a 'community' (the classroom in this case).

Each proof presentation was slightly different and some were more mathematically rigorous than others, but all students had started the process of producing mathematical proofs. Students when interviewed explicitly said that they valued the use of ICT tools, which allowed them to progressively develop their mathematical proofs. Within this context writing draft proofs on the screen in dynamic geometry had enabled them to begin to externally represent their proto-proofs which gradually evolved into more formal and theoretically informed proofs. As Rick explained, constructing and undoing were an important part of this process: 'The thing was, much of our project was wrong; it wasn't wrong but large amounts of it were quite bad. So had we been doing it on paper it would have taken us longer to get nowhere, so it meant we could just delete it and start again. We used undo a lot. (final interview)

The students explained to Marnie why writing in PowerPoint had been valuable:

Marnie: 'We wouldn't have liked to do that on pencil and paper, Miss', 'If we'd had to do that it would have got really messy' – was one of the comments. 'If we'd had to do that we would have kept having to rub it out and we'd have got bored, and it would have been so time consuming', 'And it would have just been dreadful' – one of them said, in that sort of term.

(Final interview)

Concluding remarks

One of the main results of the InterActive Education Project was that effective teaching and learning with ICT involves finding ways of building bridges between 'individual and idiosyncratic' and 'common' knowledge. This is because students can work with ICT for extended periods of time, investigating their own questions and experimenting with ideas in an interactive way. Whereas this relates to the power and potential of ICT for learning, it can also lead to the construction of idiosyncratic knowledge which is at odds with the intended learning.

This is exemplified by the work in Pat and Marnie's classrooms, where we can see from students' interactions with the computer that they sometimes construct mathematical knowledge which is at odds with the intended learning. For example, 'a parallelogram is the colour turquoise, measuring is proof'. Interestingly, because whole-class work is the only way of putting these conceptions out in the open, making them visible, enabling them to be discussed by other students and the teacher, whole-class work is the only way of developing a mathematical community of inquiry in which students become explicitly aware of new mathematical objects and new mathematical tools. Whole-class work becomes even more important when students are working individually or in pairs at the computer.

Notes

1. In England the results of standard assessment test (SATs) for all primary and secondary schools are published annually. Schools which are under-achieving relative to the national norm are under considerable pressure to raise the level of attainment of students. Marnie Weeden now works as the Head of Mathematics in the City Academy in Bristol.
2. The mathematics design team of the InterActive Education Project worked together over a period of two years, meeting at the university for approximately 15 days (sometimes made up of half days) throughout this period.
3. For example as part of the University of Bristol's MEd course 'Learning Mathematics with New Technologies', http://www.bris.ac.uk/education/

programmes/masters/med/pathways/maths, and as a co-director of the ESRC Microworlds' Project (Sutherland et al. 1991).
4. Software from the UK's National Numeracy Strategy; www.standards.dfes. gov.uk/numeracy/.
5. The phrase mathematical microworld is used here to mean a designed environment in which it is likely that students will bump into, engage with and learn the intended mathematical knowledge. For further discussion of this see Balacheff and Sutherland (1994).
6. Education Action Zones allow local partnerships – schools, parents, the community, businesses and local authorities – to find radical and innovative solutions to their problems: 'We are committed to seeing them work, and each gets up to £1 million a year for at least three years, a quarter of this from business partners. The important point is not the extra money but how they spend it to improve. They will need to change attitudes and approaches in order to seek solutions to long standing problems, working with businesses and other partners. They must set themselves demanding targets for improvement' (Tony Blair, January 1999).
7. In particular the Key Stage 3 results for Marnie's Year 9 (13–14) class were higher than predicted.
8. http://www.standards.dfes.gov.uk/primary.
9. http://www.standards.dfes.gov.uk/secondary.
10. This relates to how the InterActive Project was organized and is discussed more fully in Chapter 5.
11. The diagnostic assessment instrument was developed by Hoyles and Küchemann as part of the Proof Project (http://www.theproofproject.org/).
12. Marnie Weeden had trained to become a teacher on the University of Bristol's PGCE (Post Graduate Certificate in Education) course and her tutor had been Laurinda Brown (for more information on Laurinda's work in mathematics education see http://www.bris.ac.uk/education/people/academicstaff/edleb). Laurinda Brown is currently the Editor of *The Learning of Mathematics*, FLM Publishing Association, Canada.
13. Marnie had been influenced by the work of John Mason (http://cme.open. ac.uk/JHMFurthPartics.htm).
14. Two video cameras were used in the classroom, one focusing on the whole class and the other focusing on a pair of students.
15. Two pairs of students were video recorded during each session, one higher-attaining pair and one lower-attaining pair. These were obtained by asking the teacher to rank the students according to their attainment in class and we then divided this list into thirds. Chantale was chosen from the top third of ranked students and she worked with Candice throughout the six sessions. Zacharias was chosen from the bottom third and he worked with Michael throughout the six session. Chantale had been targeted, by the class teacher, to obtain Level 4 in the Stage 2 mathematics tests and Zacharias had been targeted to obtain Level 3c.

9 Theory as a Way of Seeing

> The one idea I have been advocating that seems to be at least potentially acceptable to a wide range of critics is the idea of regarding theories and the like as tools ... The tool idea is not hard to grasp and it would seem to be safe from the worst excesses of relativism. No one would claim that every tool is as good as every other. The value of a tool is relative. But always relative to some purpose.
>
> (Bereiter 2002: 476)

Introductory remarks

It sometimes seems as if the world is divided into those people who feel more comfortable living in the world of practice and those who feel more comfortable living in the world of theory. Teachers by the nature of their work predominantly live in the world of practice, and educational researchers tend to live in the world of theory. What I hope for is that in the future these boundaries will become more permeable, enabling teachers and researchers to shift between these two worlds. More importantly, I believe that mathematics education research is not likely to impact on practice until we reach a time when the construction of theories for teaching and learning mathematics emerges from partnerships between teachers and researchers.

Why am I arguing this? First the current situation, which exists in many countries around the world, where researchers alone construct theory has not in general resulted in teachers making use of this work. I have worked for many years as a mathematics education researcher, working with some of the foremost research teams in the world. Yet in my day-to-day encounters with mathematics teachers very few of them have bumped into the work which has been produced by these teams. The International Group for the Psychology of Mathematics Education[1] meets annually, producing more and more research papers each year, research which is having very little impact on the world of teaching and learning mathematics. The second reason why I am arguing for more permeable boundaries is that when groups of mathematics teachers engage with theoretical perspectives, they are able to use theory in order to both illuminate their own practices and to produce new theory for transforming practice. Finally the third reason is that if theory production remains within the domain of academics there will always be a tendency to overlook the most important aspect of teachers' work, namely thinking in the moment and responding contingently and creatively to what students bring to the mathematics classroom.

Culture and mathematics learning

As I argued in Chapter 2 mathematics teachers are always working within a local mathematics education culture, the culture within their school, situated within regional and national mathematics education cultures. People in this local culture share core values and beliefs which may not be shared by members of a different local mathematics education culture. These relate to values and beliefs about mathematics, about learning, about teaching, and about students' capabilities. For example, teachers in primary schools are likely to share different beliefs about learning from teachers in secondary schools. Teachers in state schools are likely to share different values and beliefs from teachers in private schools. Mathematics teachers are also working within a regional or national policy system and these policies impact on the culture at the level of the classroom. For example, assessment policies influence the intended mathematical learning in the classroom.

A mathematics education culture overlaps with the culture of mathematicians, drawing on the language and symbols of mathematicians, but also constructing its own language and symbols for particular teaching and learning purposes. There is inevitably an inter-relationship between school mathematics and the mathematics of the academy which works in both directions, with the academy influencing schools and vice versa.

In imperceptible ways a mathematics education culture and the members of the culture mutually change over time as well as from place to place. The mathematics education I experienced as a student in a grammar school[2] in the 1960s is different from the mathematics education my daughter experienced in a comprehensive school[3] in the 1980s and different again from that which young people are experiencing in school nowadays. The mathematics education culture in a secondary school is different from the mathematics education culture in a primary school.[4]

Awareness of working within a mathematics education culture can help in the unpacking of why we do things in certain ways. For example why do mathematics teachers in the UK teach students to solve equations using a trial-and-refinement approach? Why do teachers in France and Italy draw on mathematical theorems (for example Thale's theorem)[5] that English teachers are not aware of? Why do textbook writers in some countries make extensive use of multiple ways of representing mathematics whereas textbook writers in other countries appear to eschew such representations? Questioning and coming to understand aspects of the mathematics education culture which frames our work can empower us to change aspects of teaching mathematics which impact on learning.

Mathematical tools

A key concept from socio-cultural theory is the idea that all human activity is mediated by tools. These tools, invented by people living in particular cultures, are potentially transformative, that is, they enable people to do things which they could not readily do without such tools. Any mathematical tool emerges from a particular historical and cultural context, and carries with it the provenance of this culture. As Pea (1993) points out the inventions of Leibnitz's calculus and Descartes' coordinate graphs are in some ways carriers of the residual intelligence of those who invented them.

All cultures have developed mathematical tools. The Maya in Mexico developed numerals and a calendar system. The Incas in Peru developed the *quipu*, a device for recording numbers in a decimal system. The Yoruba in south-western Nigeria developed a base 20 counting system. The Egyptians developed a system for representing and manipulating fractions, and the Chinese developed a system for representing and manipulating negative numbers.[6] All of these mathematical tools emerged from an interplay between pragmatic needs and symbolic invention, deeply rooted in and influenced by the corresponding socio-cultural settings.

As Perkins (1993) has argued so convincingly, in the world outside school people use tools all the time. He coined the phrase person-plus-tool to emphasize the ineluctable tool-using aspect of human activity. Mathematical algorithms are examples of such symbolic tools as is the calculator. Interestingly both mathematical algorithms and the calculator have been devalued by educators for similar reasons, namely that they do some of the work for us. Paradoxically the very power of the tool is that it does some work for us, allowing us to produce things which we could not produce without the tool. And this is the very reason why it becomes controversial to educators. This suggests that it is important to analyse the potential affordances of mathematical tools, the mathematical work we want them to do for us and the mathematical work we want students to do for themselves. This is where the world inside school is different from the world outside school. The focus in school is more about learning particular ideas and the focus outside school is more about getting things done, solving problems. So for example if students at school use a calculator to solve a 'multiplication problem' using repeated addition, they may be solving the problem but they may not be learning about multiplication.

Work inside school also differs in another respect from work outside school. Tools are sometimes developed for purely pedagogical purposes: they exist only in the world of education. This is illustrated by the 'empty number line' which was developed by Freudenthal (1973) to support the development of number sense. The number line has been designed to support students to do something which would not be possible without the use of such a tool. But here the aim is for students to internalize or appropriate the tool, to eventually be able to 'imagine with the tool', even when the tool is no longer present in a material form. Thus there are two distinct practices with mathematical tools. In the first there is no intention to remove the tool (what Salomon (1993) calls effects-with) as for example when I use Excel to construct a complex budget. In the second the aim is to remove the tool (what Salomon calls effects-of). Here the focus in on the residue left behind when the tool is removed. The tool is used as a temporary scaffold on the path to mathematical learning. For example, the use of the empty number line can be seen as the creation of a new functional learning system for students, aiding students to create a new mental object of number.[7] Interestingly when the calculator was 'banned' from English tests some students continued to use the 'trial-and-refinement' approach developed with the calculator even when solving problems with paper and pencil providing further evidence that there can be a residue left behind when a tool is removed (see for example Figure 9.1).

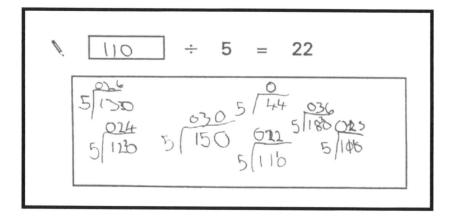

Figure 9.1 Trial-and-refinement approach to division

The idea of embodying conceptual mathematical ideas in concrete materials has a long history in the primary school. Dienes (1960) for example developed an elaborate system of representations for teaching place value which was used extensively in British primary schools in the 1960s and 70s. However, Brousseau (1997) has rather convincingly argued that only those teachers who understand the theoretical thinking behind the development of the materials are likely to use them for effective mathematical learning.

Writing about and communicating mathematics is a central aspect of mathematicians' work and arguably an important aspect of school mathematics. Interestingly there has been very little research on the role of tools in writing mathematics, particularly with respect to the work of mathematicians. Recently Misfeldt (2005) categorized the ways in which mathematicians use media when writing, which includes writing for trying out ideas and seeing connections, writing for storing information for later retrieval, writing for communication with fellow collaborators and writing for the scientific production of a paper. He found that mathematicians tend to use different media (both digital and non-digital) for these different processes. For example, many mathematicians used paper and pencil for trying out ideas and seeing connections, e-mail for communication purposes and LateX[8] for the production of papers. However, Misfeldt also pointed out that there are differences between mathematicians in their choice of tools for writing. He also argued that:

> So long as pen and paper are the primary support for one or more of the functions in mathematical writing amongst researchers it makes sense for students to have access to this medium at all times. Doing mathematics in a computer lab without any desk space can be a problem if some essential work is done with a pen and a piece of paper.
>
> (p. 40)

What all this suggests is that within school mathematics it is important to identify which tools are the focus of mathematical learning, which are being introduced as a scaffold in the process of mathematical learning and which are being used as tools for writing and communicating about mathematical ideas. With the increasing prevalence of digital mathematical tools it is also important to identify the relative affordances of digital and non-digital tools, understanding our reasons for using digital tools in the mathematics classroom. For example what can we do with paper-and-pencil graphing that we cannot do with a digital graph-plotting package and vice versa? Such knowledge will enable teachers and students to become more resourceful, more aware of which tool is the most effective for which situation, and also to become more aware of when they might be continuing to use the 'residue' of a tool in their imagination even when it is no longer present.

Appropriating and appropriate mathematics

How we view the development of mathematical knowledge influences our view of teaching and learning. Some people view this development from a perspective of 'earlier is more primitive' and later is 'more sophisticated'. This has been called 'hererogeneity as genetic hierarchy'.[9] From this point of view a return to an earlier approach to solving a problem is viewed as regression, and learning mathematics is conceptualized as progressively correcting misconceptions. Brousseau (1997: 85) argues that 'this is why there must be a sufficient flow of new situations which it cannot assimilate, which will destabilise it, make it ineffective, useless, wrong; which necessitate reconsidering it or rejecting it, forgetting it, cutting it up – until its final manifestation'.

This view of knowledge development has led many mathematics education researchers to search for what could be called 'the holy grail' of mathematical problem situations, which if adequately crafted will almost inevitably lead students to construct the intended mathematical knowledge. This approach has sometimes been accompanied by a belief that students will be able to 'discover' the intended mathematical knowledge through engagement with the problem alone. This approach prioritizes the view of the individual as a 'lone scientist' and downplays the role which culture and community play in the construction of knowledge. For example, problembased approaches to learning algebra tend to assume that if students are presented with what are called algebra problems then students will need to use algebra to solve such problem. However, for any so called algebra problem it is always possible to solve it with a non-algebraic approach,[10] for any so called multiplication problem it is possible to solve it through repeated addition.

This suggests that it important to analyse the relationship between the problem, the available tools and the problem-solving approach, all of which will be situated within a particular mathematics education culture. For example when 10-year-old students were presented with the following problem in a test in which the calculator was banned, many used a trial-and-refinement approach which they had developed when using a calculator (Figure 9.1). They used a 'repeated division' approach to find the number which when divided by 5 produces 22.

French students of a similar age solved the same problem by inverting the operation, that is by multiplying 22 by 5.[11] It is very likely that those who prepared this test item intended students to invert the operations, but the fact that British students (even when the calculator was not present) used a much less efficient strategy of 'repeated division' shows how creative people are in finding 'any approach' to solving a mathematical problem. This suggests that the ways in which students use calculators in the classroom are influenced as much by the mathematics education culture as by the tool itself.

Another perspective on the construction of knowledge assumes that there is no inherent ranking of tools in their power with respect to particular problem situations. This has been called 'nongenetic heterogeneity'. This perspective, at least implicitly, has been dominant within the British mathematics education culture for many years. From this point of view all approaches to solving a problem are valued equally. Consider an example taken from a teacher's guide to a popular primary school mathematics text-book (Figure 9.2). The teacher's guide suggests that pupils should be encouraged to solve the presented problem in many ways: 'Ask each child to find his/her own way to calculate the exact answers, using paper-and-pencil methods, and then to check the answer with the calculator'. Interestingly the guide does not differentiate between the use of the two tools 'paper and pencil' and 'calculator' although (as discussed earlier) the approach to solving the problem could very well be different with each different tool. In this teacher's guide the standard algorithm is presented as one of a range of methods. Each method is not considered for its relative efficiency.

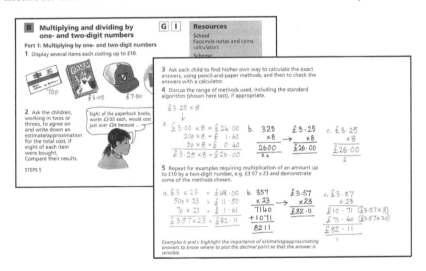

Figure 9.2 Teaching multiplication to 7–8-year-olds – excerpt from teacher's guide to one of the most popular schemes in the UK

I suggest that this approach to the development of mathematical knowledge is problematic. From this perspective there would be no need or desire to learn new mathematical tools, if the old tools were adequate or good enough.

The perspective on knowledge development which I believe is the most valuable, acknowledges that different forms of cognitive functioning emerge at different periods, but that the later ones are not inherently more powerful than the earlier ones. Which tool is the most efficient relates to the problem situation. This has been called 'heterogeneity despite genetic hierarchy'. From this point of view it becomes possible to talk about common-sense thinking, scientific thinking, artistic thinking where 'common sense is better for one sphere of life, science for another, philosophic criticism for a third' (Wertsch 1991: 101). Although common-sense or informal thinking is likely to develop before scientific thinking it is not necessarily a less efficient or powerful tool for solving a particular problem. Whereas different mathematical tools may be acquired at different developmental stages (for example arithmetic before algebra) there is no inherent ranking of a tool with respect to power and efficiency. So algebra is not necessarily a more powerful tool for solving a particular problem, but it is a more powerful tool within some problem situation. This perspective fits with Vygotsky's suggestion that earlier forms of knowing are not always transformed and incorporated into later forms; they co-exist, they do not have to be replaced and eradicated. This also suggests that more formal mathematical concepts do not grow naturally out of everyday concepts; they require a qualitative shift of attention.

The implications of taking this later perspective when teaching mathematics is that it becomes important to address openly in the classroom the issue that different mathematical tools can be more appropriate for use in different situations. This leads to the idea of a tool-kit approach to learning mathematics, in which teachers and students become aware of which tools are relatively powerful and efficacious in which problem situations:

> A tool kit approach allows group and contextual differences in mediated action to be understood in terms of the array of mediational means to which people have access and the patterns of choice they manifest in selecting a particular means for a particular occasion.
>
> (Wertsch 1991: 94)

Wertsch introduces the idea of privileging: 'Privileging refers to the fact that one mediational means, such as a social language, is viewed as being more appropriate or efficacious than others in a particular sociocultural setting' (p. 124). Wertsch argues that the patterns of privileging are accessible to conscious reflection and hence to change. I think this idea is an important one for the mathematics classroom. Teachers and students can become aware of which mathematical tool they are privileging and why. Teachers can explicitly explain to students why they have decided to privilege a particular tool instead of others, because this will result in increased efficacy for certain types of problems and certain types of situations.

Teaching, tools and transformation

If each new tool potentially transforms what a person can do, the question of who is given access to which new tools becomes an important one to address. However, it is also important to understand that a new tool is only potentially transformative. Whether or not a new tool is actually transformative relates to the way it is used, which relates to the culture in which it is used, which relates to the role of the teacher in the classroom. There is nothing within the tool itself which causes transformation to happen, as evidenced by the multitude of students who have never understood the point of learning algebra. Interestingly when it comes to digital tools there is a tendency for policy makers around the world to believe that the mere introduction of the tool in the classroom will of itself lead to changes in the way in which students learn mathematics.

Tools are only transformative if the people using them can 'see' the potential for transformation. In general it is not easy to 'see' the potential of new mathematical tools, without the support of another person who, as it were, opens your eyes or focuses your attention on what is possible. This is the case for both non-digital and digital tools. For example, it would be very difficult for someone to 'see' the potential of the Cartesian coordinate system without the support of someone who knows how and why to use the system. Similarly it would be very difficult for someone (teachers or students) to see the potential of dynamic geometry software for doing and learning mathematics. The Cartesian coordinate system and dynamic geometry are relatively opaque tools.

Almost all mathematical tools are relatively opaque, in contrast to a whole range of tools which have been designed with relatively 'transparent'[12] interfaces, for example the wrist watch. This is one of the main reasons why teachers are key to introducing new mathematical tools into the classroom, enabling students to see the potential of and learn about new mathematical tools. A re-reading of the way in which Alf Coles introduces 11–12-year-old students to symbolic algebra shows how he incessantly and often imperceptibly pushes students into new ways of seeing, new ways of knowing and new ways of theorizing (Chapter 5).

From a socio-cultural perspective it is important to emphasize that all human activity is mediated by people as well as being mediated by material and symbolic tools. Teachers as more-knowledgeable others are central to mathematical learning in schools. As Bruner (1996: 84) so eloquently pointed out:

> No educational reform can get off the ground without an adult actively and honestly participating – a teacher willing and prepared

to give and share aid, to comfort and to scaffold. Learning in its full complexity involves the creation and negotiation of meaning in a larger culture, and the teacher is the vicar of the culture at large. You cannot teacher-proof a curriculum any more than you can parent-proof a family.

How then should a teacher act in the classroom? We now know that the more traditional approaches to teaching in which the teacher attempts to transmit knowledge through 'telling' are not productive. We also know that the more progressive student-centred approaches in which students are expected to discover mathematics for themselves are also not productive. Interestingly many teachers probably already operate in what could be called a middle-ground in which there is discussion and dialogue between students and teachers and a joint construction of knowledge. We are beginning to understand more from comparative studies of mathematics classrooms around the world that what is happening at the level of the micro-dynamics of the classroom is often very different from what a superficial reading of the teacher and students' positioning can tell us. So for example both Alf (Chapter 5) and Simon (Chapter 4) spend periods of time at the front of the class in what could be considered a traditional set-up, but the actual discussion and interchange between students in these classroom is very different from the classic 'question, answer, response' of traditional classrooms. What is being created in these classroom is a community in which the work of the whole class becomes more than the sum of the individual parts, a community of mathematics learners.

Language, community and mathematical learners

In the previous sections of this chapter I emphasized the role of digital and non-digital, material and symbolic mathematical tools. I also emphasized the role of mathematics teachers as gateways to the world of mathematics. In this section I discuss the ways in which the community of students also contribute to what is learned in the mathematics classroom. As discussed already in Chapter 3 students actively construct knowledge, drawing on what they already know and believe. They come to a classroom as knowing beings. They bring to the classroom a diversity of previous learning experiences, which can be exploited by the teacher.

How then can a teacher face and make sense of this diversity? Making it open, making it visible, pulling it together into a viable collective whole in which students begin to share meanings and communicate together. This is how all scientific communities behave, including the scientific community of mathematicians. They behave 'as if' they are talking the same mathematical language, and through this process come to construct shared meaning. From a Vygotskian perspective:

> it is possible for a child to produce seemingly appropriate communication behaviour before recognising all aspects of its significance as understood by more experienced members of the culture ... In more informal terms our claim is that children can say more than they realise and it is through coming to understand what is meant by what is said that their cognitive skills develop.
>
> (Wertsch and Stone 1985: 167)

If all human action is mediated by tools then, as Cole and Engestrom (1993) have pointed out, the master tool is language. All mathematics is shot through with language, all mathematical learning is inextricably linked to the use of natural language. And one aspect of the classroom which has long been ignored, possibly as a reaction to the more traditional role of the teacher is the role of imitation. Bauersfeld (1995: 283) has drawn attention to the fact that:

> For too long education had neglected the functioning of imitative learning, which indeed happens in every classroom as the most common form of learning in a culture (Tomasello, Kruger & Ratner, 1993). As an agent of the embedding culture, the teacher functions as a peer with a special mission and power in the classroom culture. The teacher therefore has to take special care of the richness of the classroom culture – rich in offers, challenges, alternatives and models, including languaging.

Wertsch (1991: 59) also focuses on the importance of languaging, and drawing on the work of Bahktin (1981: 293–4) considers different types of language genres to be key parts of a tool-kit approach:

> The word in language is half someone else's. It becomes one's own only when the speaker populates it with his own intention, his own accent, when he appropriates the word, adapting it to his own semantic and expressive intention. Prior to this moment of appropriation, the word does not exist in a neutral language and impersonal language (it is not, after all, out of a dictionary that the speaker gets his words!), but rather it exists in other people's mouths, in other people's concrete contexts, serving other people's intentions: it is from there that one must take the word and make it one's own.

The use of language in the mathematics classroom 'is a very strict game with strange rules about what is allowed and what is not, and the child's only access to this new subculture is active participation' (Bauersfeld 1995: 285). Teachers play a key role in inducting students to develop shared meanings of mathematical language (see the way in which Alf Coles does this in Chapter 5). Creating a community of mathematics-speaking people is the only way in which young people will ever be able to speak and write this 'strange' mathematical language. Bauersfeld suggests that what is important here is that the teacher maintains a classroom culture in which students have as many chances as possible to present their ideas and conjectures, for feedback from other members of the class and from the teacher, not only verbal feedback but through actions and demonstrations.

> Children pick up elements of languaging, imitate and try them when communicating in similar situations, change the ascriptions of meaning according to the experienced reactions and thus in time learn to fill these imitated elements with certain taken-as-shared meanings specific to the situation.
>
> (p. 287)

What I am trying to emphasize here is that the teacher is a gateway to the world of mathematical language and the world of mathematical tools. In other words the teacher is a key agent for creating a mathematical micro-culture in the classroom. But the activities and the 'languaging' of the students in the classroom are also a constituent part of this culture. What the teacher creates is inter-dependent on what the students bring to the classroom. For example, when Simon worked with his class of 8–10-year-old students the mathematics which was constructed was very much influenced by Simon's orchestration of the class, but it was also influenced by the students' expertise and also their ability to play with the digital tool and discover new functionalities which Simon had not intended to be the focus of the lesson (see Chapter 5).

Why theory?

In the UK there has been a tendency to 'protect' teachers from the theorizing process. Curriculum documents and strategies make statements which are not supported by theoretical explanations. When a theoretical construct is used it is used out of context as in the following example, taken from advice given by the Qualifications and Curriculum Authority:[13]

> The teacher's role in discussion is to encourage the articulation of intuitive viewpoints and to challenge with alternative viewpoints. By fostering cognitive conflict, the teacher can help learners to re-

evaluate their ideas. Discussion will help pupils to expose their beliefs and then to reconstruct and develop their own concepts – to learn from their mistakes.

The explanation for this statement is situated within the authority of the text. The fact that the idea of 'cognitive conflict' derives from a Piagetian perspective is hidden from the reader.

Getting a handle on a theoretical perspective is not easy and, in my opinion, the only way forward is for communities of teachers and researchers to build up a culture of teaching and learning mathematics which is framed by theory. This involves working in partnership, and as I discussed in previous chapters, the process of designing for learning can be threaded through with a developing awareness of theory. The alternative, namely protecting teachers from educational theory would be to treat teachers as technicians who are not expected to challenge and problematize. This in its turn is likely to lead to teachers treating their students in similar ways, likely to lead to a dumbing-down of the student community.

Notes

1. See http://www.igpme.org/.
2. Between 1944 and the mid 1960s, most local authorities in England operated a system of grammar, technical and secondary modern schools, with pupils being allocated to schools on the basis of their performance in 11-plus examinations. Grammar schools selected pupils on the basis of their 11-plus examinations, providing an academic course from age 11 to 16 or 18.
3. Nowadays the main type of secondary school, attended by 86.8 per cent of secondary pupils in England (100 per cent in Wales). Comprehensives cater for children of all abilities.
4. See Brown and Coles (2003).
5. If several parallel straight lines are cut by two transversal lines, the ratio of any two segments of one of these transversals is equal to the ratio of the corresponding segments of the other transversal.
6. For further discussion of this see Joseph (1992).
7. For further discussion of this see Beishuizen (1999).
8. LateX is a typesetting system widely used within the mathematical community.
9. For further discussion of these ideas see Wertsch (1991) and Chapter 5.
10. See Chapter 6 for further discussion of this.
11. See Osborn (1998) for further discussion of this.
12. Andy Clark (2003: 28) defines a *transparent technology* as 'a technology that is so well fitted to, and integrated with, our own lives, biological capacities, and

projects as to become almost invisible in use. An *opaque technology*, by contrast, is one that keeps tripping the user up, requires skills and capacities that do not come naturally to the biological organism, and thus remains the focus of attention even during routine problem-solving activity'.

13. The Qualifications and Curriculum Authority (QCA) in England – see http://www.qca.org.uk/.

10 Integrating Research, Policy and Practice

In science the analysis into elements ought to be replaced by analysis which reduces a complex unity, a complex whole to its units. We have said that, unlike elements, these units represent such products which do not lose any of the properties which are characteristic of the whole, but which manage to retain, in the manner of the most elementary form the properties inherent in the whole.

(Vygotsky 1994: 342)

Introductory remarks

Learning mathematics is a complex and messy process, a process which takes time and which cannot be reduced to a rote-like focus on transmitting bits of knowledge. Learning mathematics requires an educational system which supports and does not inhibit good teaching, an educational system which tries to understand the theories behind the reforms it imposes on teachers and is honest about what is known and what is not yet known about teaching and learning mathematics.

In the case of mathematics theoretical knowledge has developed over centuries. In the case of teaching and learning mathematics we are on much more shaky theoretical grounds. Although this book has been influenced by a particular socio-cultural approach to teaching and learning, this theoretical perspective still needs long-term evaluation and development in classroom situations. In other words we do not yet know (and may never know) enough to be dogmatic about teaching and learning mathematics. But we do know enough to provide reasoned explanations for curriculum reforms which draw to a certain extent on theoretical ideas.

So whereas I have argued against the pervasive use of 'trial and improvement' for solving mathematics problems I am now going to argue for a 'trial-and-improvement' approach to teaching and learning mathematics. In this approach the teacher modifies what he/she does in response to feedback on students' learning. In this approach teachers are enabled practitioners who have themselves been educated in a national system which emphasizes challenge and explanation.

Unintended effects of educational reforms

Educational reforms often have unintended and unpredictable effects on classroom practices of teaching and learning. Throughout the 1980s and early 1990s many changes were made to school mathematics in the UK. Changes were made to the whole system. The National Curriculum, textbooks and assessment approaches were all transformed with the expectation that young people would become more successful at using mathematics in a range of situations, both outside school and in other 'school' subjects.[1] The various strands of the recommendations all centred around the idea of making mathematics more meaningful for the majority. Influenced by research at the time there was a big push to encourage teachers to value the knowledge children bring to the classroom and thus draw on their informal methods. These reforms do not appear to have resulted in the desired outcomes.

The argument for taking more account of children's methods related to the conclusion that children 'frequently tackle mathematics problems with methods that have little or nothing to do with what has been taught' (Küchemann 1981: 118). A view emerged that individualized learning would be more effective than whole-class teaching. This student-centred approach also influenced the view that students should be encouraged to develop informal methods. Interestingly as I discussed in Chapter 9 informal methods often became the taught and thus institutionalized method.[2]

Much of classical school algebra had involved teaching standard algorithms for solving equations. These standard algorithms became associated with traditional and rote ways of teaching, which were perceived as being in opposition to relevance and understanding. The unintended effects of this celebrating of relevance and student-centred approaches was that for a while in the UK the majority of students had very little experience of 'traditional' algebra. Interestingly it is now increasingly recognized that to develop symbol sense in mathematics it is sometimes necessary to postpone a quest for meaning and to 'live with partial understandings for long periods of time, until meanings are connected and a larger picture emerges' (Arcavi 2005: 45).

In the UK curriculum reforms have not usually been accompanied by any elaborated explanation of the reasons for these reforms. Teachers are treated almost as technicians who do not need to know about theory and explanation. Interestingly this is not the case in all countries around the world. For example, in The Netherlands extensive reforms have been accompanied by an evolving theoretical perspective on teaching and learning mathematics, called Realistic Mathematics Education and influenced by the work of Freudenthal.[3]

Interestingly, and worryingly, individualized learning is currently being reinvented by policy makers and politicians as personalized learning.[4] This seems to relate to a rather pervasive idea that increased use of ICT in schools will or should result in more 'individualized' approaches to learning. However, a playing-down of the role of the teacher accompanied by a devolving of the responsibility of teaching and learning to ICT will not lead to enhanced mathematical learning for students.

Teachers as enabled professionals

Throughout this book I have argued for the development of networked groups of teachers and researchers who work together to design mathematics learning initiatives. This is what Peter John (2006: 273) has called the enabled professional, 'one who has the capacity to respond to changing conditions, anticipate future technologies, and re-define their practice so that they are enabled rather than constrained by external policy agendas'. Working with colleagues in the InterActive Education Project we developed a process of innovation which differs in a number of ways from other curriculum development and action research projects:

> Using the concept of interacting and interpenetrating 'layers of community' enables us to understand how different communities of practice supported the development of what we term the 'enabled professional' and to identify some of the factors that impeded it. While we would argue strongly that all teachers should be given time for reflection, we recognise that the privileged conditions under which this research was carried out are unlikely to be capable of exact duplication. We should, though, focus on the central features that underpinned this professional development process:
>
> - a reduction of a sense of isolation, contact with others who share your professional interests and concerns;
> - interaction that involves knowledge exchange as the basis for knowledge transformation;
> - encouragement to take risks combined with support in analysing why things go wrong and how they might improve.
>
> (John 2006: 273)

The idea of layered communities recognizes the different type of work which needs to take place across the different layers. As discussed in Chapter 7 the work of the micro-level community is concerned with design and realization at the level of the classroom. The work of the meso-level community is concerned with research-informed design. The work of the macro-community is concerned explicitly with theory development. Importantly there is omni-directional knowledge movement across the layers, with knowledge, ideas and practices extending upwards, downwards, across and around the various communities. This model merges professional development and research, and differs from action research in its emphasis on theorizing which is a major aspect of the work of the macro-level community.

This model emphasizes the importance of knowledge exchange. Unfortunately in the workplace (which includes schools and universities) people have a tendency to hold on to know-how because they fear that their work might become redundant if they transform this know-how into tangible knowledge objects which can be used by other professionals. The situation is complex because personal knowledge networks play an important role in the functioning of an organization, yet they can be viewed with suspicion as the knowledge within them is not available to the organisation.[5] Hargreaves (2003) argues that the school system will only be transformed when knowledge is shared between schools and teachers. He uses the phrase 'innovation network' to describe such a horizonal communication of knowledge, and believes that ICT will play a key role in the transformation of educational knowledge. This network model emphasizes the way in which ideas are developed from the bottom up and contrasts with a more traditional view of expertise as being embodied within an 'expert'. However, such transformation in the creation and communication of knowledge is not likely to occur as long as teachers reify craft wisdom at the expense of more formal, research-warranted knowledge. Such transformation is not likely to occur until teachers are enabled to continue to develop their practice as part of a life-long professional development programme.

This leads to a consideration of the role of technology in the generation and transformation of knowledge. Here socio-cultural theory enables us to see that all human activity is mediated by tools and technologies. Whereas traditionally knowledge exchanges were predominantly carried out through face-to-face exchanges between people, new digital tools enable knowledge to be created in an a-temporal and distributed way, reducing the need for joint work to take place at the same time and in the same place. Moreover the convergence of text, image and sound within new media, can break down the dominance of propositional knowledge. In this sense 'digital tools have the potential to enfranchise marginalised groups as user-friendly interfaces operate with more subtle levels of cultural embededness than interfaces based on abstract commands' (The New London Group 1996: 11). This, it has been argued relates to the new social relationships of work:

> whereas the old Fordist organisation depended upon clear, precise and formal systems of command such as written memos and the supervisor's orders, effective teamwork depends to a much greater extent on informal, oral and interpersonal discourse. This

informality also translates into hybrid and interpersonally sensitive written forms, such as electronic mail.

(p. 12)

The creation of knowledge is also inextricably linked to the representation of knowledge, and new digital technologies are being developed for creating and communicating knowledge, as illustrated by the remarkable example of *wikipedia* – an on-line encyclopedia which is constructed in a bottom-up way.[6] Digital video also enables teachers and researchers to experiment with new ways of representing and communicating teachers' professional knowledge so that it connects more readily with teachers' discourses. In this way digital video can be used to provide teachers with realistic 'portraits of practice' as illustrated by this statement:

> Most of us when we look at ICT we go for what's safe. We go to what we know. Whereas this sometimes is not particularly safe – I like that. Have a go and get it wrong. The video was the important thing – watching myself teach and being able to see kids when I'm not there. I had a very negative attitude to being observed – OfSTED and others – but this allowed me to sit and watch and be comfortable with it ... it's an important process. I can now refine my teaching ... sit back and reflect properly. I never had the chance and video made it happen.
> (Teacher-partner in InterActive Education Project)

A question of scale

I will end this book by introducing a question which has preoccupied me for many years and introducing an image (Figure 10.1) which I use as a tool to think about this question. Can we understand the complexity of a mathematics classroom by analysing any excerpt of a lesson? In other words, can we think about teaching and learning in the classroom as a fractal which is scale independent, which does not become simpler when magnified or reduced. As Davis (2004: 192) has pointed out:

> The value of fractal geometry to studies of education is just beginning to be demonstrated. For example, in terms of description, the notion of scale independence and self-similarity are useful for making sense of the levelled and embedded natures of individuals, social collectives, bodies of knowledge, cultures and societies.

When faced with endless video recordings of one mathematics teacher's work in the classroom I mostly believe that studying any part will illuminate the

Figure 10.1 A self-similar structure

whole which is the essence of this teacher's way of teaching for learning mathematics. I leave it to others to take up the methodological challenge of showing that this is the case.

Notes

1. These reforms were influenced by the Cockroft Report (1982) and also related to the introduction of a national curriculum in England and Wales. For more discussion on the reforms see Johnson and Millett (1996). For a critique of the introduction of the National Curriculum in England and Wales see Dowling and Noss (1990).
2. For further discussion of this see the Royal Society/JMC Report (1997). This report is available at http://www.royalsoc.ac.uk/.
3. For more discussion on Realistic Mathematics Education see Freudenthal (1991) and Gravemeijer (1994).
4. For a discussion of personalized learning see the Department for Education and Skills (DfES) site at http://www.standards.dfes.gov.uk/personalisedlearning/. For a critical engagement with this policy perspective see *Personalised*

Learning: A Commentary by the Teaching and Learning Research Programme, www.tlrp.org.9.

5. For further discussion of this see Huysman and deWit (2003).
6. Wikipedia is only one example of a whole range of new social and knowledge technologies are being produced.

References

Abramovich, S. and Nabors, W. (1997) Spreadsheets as generators of new meanings in middle school algebra. *Computers in the Schools*, 13(1–2): 13–25.

Ainley, J. (1996) *Enriching Primary Mathematics with IT*. London: Hodder and Stoughton.

Arcavi, A. (1994) Symbol sense: the informal sense-making in formal mathematics. *For the Learning of Mathematics*, 14(3): 24–35.

Arcavi, A. (2005) Developing and using symbol sense in mathematics. *For the Learning of Mathematics*, 25(2): 42–7.

Armstrong, V. and Curran, S. (2006) Developing a collaborative model of research using digital video. *Computers and Education*, 46: 337–47.

Armstrong, V., Barnes, S., Sutherland, R., Curran, S., Mills, S. and Thompson, I. (2005) Collaborative research methodology for investigating teaching and learning: the use of interactive whiteboard technology. *Educational Review*, 57(4): 455–67.

Artigue, M. (2001) Didactic engineering in support of reasoning, explanation and proof. In *Reasoning, Explanation and Proof in School Mathematics and their Place in the Intended Curriculum*. Proceedings of the QCA International Seminar, 4–6 October 2001 Cambridge, UK QCA/02/916.

Bahktin, M.M. (1981) *The Dialogue Imagination: Four Essays by M.M. Bahktin*. Austin, TX: University of Texas Press.

Baker, D., Street, B. and Tomlin, A. (2003) Mathematics as social: understanding relationships between home and school numeracy practices. *For the Learning of Mathematics*, 23(3): 11–15.

Balacheff, N. (1988) Aspects of proof in pupils' practice of school mathematics, in D. Pimm (ed.) *Mathematics, Teachers and Children*. London: Hodder and Stoughton.

Balacheff, N. and Sutherland, R. (1994) Epistemological domain of validity of microworlds: the case of logo and cabri-géomètre, in R. Lewis and P. Mendelsohn (eds) *Lessons from Learning*, IFIP conference TGC3WG3.3, North Holland.

Bauersfeld, H. (1995) 'Language games' in the mathematics classrooom: their function and their effects, in P. Cobb and H. Bauersfeld (eds) *The Emergence of Mathematical Meaning: Interaction in Classroom Cultures*. Mahwah, NJ: Lawrence Erlbaum.

Beishuizen, M. (1999) The empty number line as a new model, in I. Thompson (ed.) *Issues in Teaching Numeracy in Primary Schools*. Buckingham: Open University Press.

Bereiter, C. (2002) *Education and Mind in the Knowledge Age*. Mahwah, NJ: Lawrence Erlbaum.

Bishop, A., Clements, J., Kietel, C., Kilpatrick, J. and Laborde, C. (eds) (1996) *International Handbook of Mathematics Education*. Amsterdam: Kluwer.

Black, P. and William, D. (1998) Assessment and classroom learning. *Assessment in Education*, March: 7–74.

Bransford, J., Brown, A. and Cocking, R. (1999) *How People Learn, Brain, Mind, Experience, and School*. Washington, DC: National Academy Press.

Brousseau, G. (1997) *Theory of Didactical Situations in Mathematics*. Amsterdam: Kluwer.

Brown, A. (1992) Design experiments: theoretical and methodological challenges in creating complex interventions in classroom settings. *The Journal of the Learning Sciences*, 2(2): 141–78.

Brown, L. (1990) *Developing Algebra*. Bristol: RLDU.

Brown, L. and Coles, A. (1999) Needing to use algebra: a case study, in Proceedings of the 21st Annual Conference, PME, Lahti.

Brown, L. and Coles, A. (2001) Natural algebraic activity, in Proceedings of the 12th ICMI Study Conference *The Future of the Teaching and Learning of Algebra*.

Brown, L. and Coles, A. (2003) Same/different: establishing a mathematical classroom culture at the transition from primary to secondary school, in R. Sutherland, G. Claxton and A. Pollard (eds) *Learning and Teaching Where Worldviews Meet*. Stoke-on-Trent: Trentham Books.

Brown, L., Sutherland, R., Winter, J. and Coles, A. (2001) Developing algebraic activity in a 'community of inquirers'. Final Report to the ESRC.

Brown, M. (1996) The context of the research – the evolution of the National Curriculum for mathematics, in Johnson, D. and Millett, A. (eds) *Implanting the Mathematics National Curriculum, Policy, Politics and Practice*, London: Paul Chapman Publishing.

Bruner, J. (1996) *The Culture of Education*. Cambridge, MA: Harvard University Press.

Clark, A. (2003) *Natural-born Cyborgs: Minds, Technologies and the Future of Human Intelligence*. Oxford: Oxford University Press.

Clarke, D. (2002) The learner's perspective study: methodology as the enactment of a theory of practice. Paper presented at the Annual Meeting of the American Educational Research Association.

Claxton, G., Pollard, A. and Sutherland, R. (2001) Fishing in the fog: conceptualising learning at the confluence of, in R. Sutherland, G. Claxton and A. Pollard (eds) *Learning and Teaching Where Worldviews Meet*. Stoke-on-Trent: Trentham Books.

Clements, D. and Battista, M. (1992) Geometry and spacial reasoning, in D.A. Grouws (ed.) *Handbook of Research on Mathematics Teaching and Learning*. Basingstoke: Macmillan.

Cobb, P. and Bauersfeld, H. (eds) (1995) *The Emergence of Mathematical Meaning: Interaction in Classroom Cultures*. Mahwah, NJ: Lawrence Erlbaum.

Cockcroft, W.H. (1982) *Mathematics Counts*. Report on the Committee of Inquiry into the Teaching of Mathematics. London: HMSO.

Cohen, J. and Stewart, I. (1994) *The Collapse of Chaos: Simple Laws in a Complex World*. London: Viking.

Cole, M. and Engestrom, Y. (1993) A cultural-historical approach to distributed cognition, in G. Salomon (ed.) *Distributed Cognition*. Cambridge: Cambridge University Press.

Coles, A. (1999) Developing a need for algebra, in *The Teacher Research Grant Scheme: Summaries of Findings 1998–1999*. London: Teacher Training Agency.

Daniels, H. (2001) *Vygotsky and Pedagogy*. London: Routledge.

Davis, B. (2004) *Inventions and Teaching: A Genealogy*. Mahwah, NJ: Lawrence Erlbaum.

Davis, B., Dennis, S. and Luce-Kapler, R. (2000) *Engaging Minds: Learning and Teaching in a Complex World*. Mahwah, NJ: Lawrence Erlbaum.

Davydov, V.V. (1991) A psychological analysis of the operation of multiplication. *Soviet Studies in Math Education, Psychological Abilities of Primary School Children in Learning Math*, 6: 8–85, NCTM.

Dienes, Z.P. (1960) *Building up Mathematics*. London: Hutchinson Educational.

Dowling, P. and Noss, R. (eds) (1990) *Mathematics versus the National Curriculum*. London: The Falmer Press.

English, I.D. (ed.) (2002) *Handbook of International Research in Mathematics Education*. Mahwah, NJ: Lawrence Erlbaum.

Facer, K., Sutherland, R., Furlong, J. and Furlong, R. (2003) *Screenplay: Childrens' Computing in the Home*. London: Routledge Falmer.

Fairclough, N. (1989) *Languages and Power*. London: Longman.

Ferguson, E. (1993) *Engineering and the Mind's Eye*. Cambridge, MA: MIT Press.

Fernandez, C. (2002) Learning from Japanese approaches to professional development: the case of lesson study. *Journal of Teacher Education*, 53(5): 390–405.

Freudenthal, H. (1973) *Mathematics as an Educational Task*. Dordrecht: Reidel.

Freudenthal, H. (1991) *Revisiting Mathematics Education: China Lectures*. Amsterdam: Kluwer.

Gallardo, A. (2001) Historical-epistemological analysis in mathematics education: two works in didactics of algebra, in R. Sutherland, T. Rojano, A. Bell and R. Lins (eds) *Perspectives on School Algebra*. Amsterdam: Kluwer.

Godwin, S. and Beswitherick, R. (2003) An investigation into the balance of prescription, experiment and play when learning about the properties of quadratic functions with ICT: research in mathematics education. *Papers of The British Society for Research into Learning Mathematics*, 5: 79–96.

Godwin, S. and Sutherland, R. (2004) Whole class technology for learning mathematics: the case of functions and graphs. *Education, Communication and Information* (ECi), 4(1): 131–52.

Goldenberg, E.P. (1988) Mathematics, metaphors, and human factors: mathematical, technical and pedagogical challenges in the educational use of graphical representation of functions. *Journal of Mathematical Behaviour*, 7: 135–73.

Goldenberg, E.P. and Cuoco, A. (1998) What is dynamic geometry, in R. Lehrer and D. Chazan (eds) *Designing Learning Environments for Developing Understanding of Geometry and Space*. Mahwah, NJ: Lawrence Erlbaum.

Gravemeijer, K. (1994) Educational development and developmental research in mathematics education. *Journal for Research in Mathematics Education*, 25(5): 443–71.

Hargreaves, D. (2003) *Education Epidemic: Transforming Secondary Schools through Innovation Networks*. Demos. Available at: www.demos.co.uk/catalogue/educationepidemic_page276.aspx.

Harries, T. and Sutherland, R. (1999) Primary school mathematics textbooks: an international comparison, in I. Thompson (ed.) *Issues Teaching Numeracy in Primary Schools*. Maidenhead: Open University Press.

Hart, K.M., Brown, M.L., Küchemann, D.E., Kerslake, D., Ruddock, G. and McCartney, M. (1981) *Children's Understanding of Mathematics: 11–16*. London: John Murray.

Healy, L. and Hoyles, C. (2001) Software tools for geometrical problem solving: potentials and pitfalls. *International Journal of Computers for Mathematical Learning*, 6: 235–56.

Healy, L. and Sutherland, R. (1990a) *Exploring Mathematics with Spreadsheets*. Hemel Hempstead: Simon and Schuster.

Healy, L. and Sutherland, R. (1990b) The use of spreadsheets within the mathematics curriculum. *International Journal of Mathematical Education in Science and Technology*, 21(6): 847–62.

Howson, G., Harries, T. and Sutherland, R. (1999) *Primary School Mathematics Textbooks: An International Study Summary*. London: QCA.

Hoyles, C. and Noss, R. (eds) (1992) *Learning Mathematics and Logo: Research and Curriculum Issues*. Cambridge, MA: MIT Press.

Hoyles, C. and Sutherland, R. (1989) *Logo Mathematics in the Classroom*. London: Routledge.

Hoyles, C., Foxman D. and Küchemann, D. (2002) *A Comparative Study of Geometry Curricula*. London: QCA.

Hoyles, C., Noss, R. and Sutherland, R. (1991) *The Ratio and Proportion Microworld*. Final report of the Microworlds Project, Volume 3, Institute of Education, University of London.

Hoyles, C., Noss, R. and Pozzi, S. (2001) Proportional reasoning in nursing practice. *Journal for Research in Mathematics Education*, 32(1): 4–27.

Huysman, M. and de Wit, D. (2003) Practices of managing knowledge sharing: towards a second wave of knowledge management. *Knowledge and Process Management*, 11(2): 81–92.

John, P. (2007) The enabled practitioner, in R. Sutherland, S. Robertson and P. John (eds) *Improving Classroom Learning with ICT*. London: Routledge.

Johnson, D. and Millett, A. (eds) (1996) *Implanting the Mathematics National Curriculum, Policy, Politics and Practice*. London: Paul Chapman Publishing.

Joseph, G.G. (1992) *The Crest of the Peacock: Non-European Roots of Mathematics.* London: Penguin Books.

Kazulin, A., Gindis, B., Ageyev, V. and Miller, S. (eds) (2003) *Vygotsky's Educational Theory in Cultural Context.* Cambridge: Cambridge University Press.

Kelly, A. (ed.) (2003) The role of design in educational research. *Educational Researcher*, 32(1): 3–4.

Kent, N. and Facer, K. (2004) Different worlds? A comparison of young people's home and school ICT use. *Journal of Computer Assisted Learning*, 20(6): 440–55.

Küchemann, D.E. (1981) Algebra, in K. Hart (ed.) *Children's Understanding of Mathematics: 11–16* London: Murray.

Laborde, C. (1993) The computer as part of the learning environment: the case of geometry, in C. Keitel and K. Ruthven (eds) *Learning from Computers: Mathematics Education and Technology.* Berlin: Springer Verlag.

Laborde, C. (2001) Integration of technology in the design of geometry tasks with Cabri-geometry, *International Journal of Computers for Mathematical Learning*, 6: 283–317.

Lave, J. (1988) *Cognition in Practice: Mind, Mathematics and Culture in Everyday Life.* Cambridge: Cambridge University Press.

Leung, F.K.S. (1995) The mathematics classroom in Beijing, Hong Kong and London. *Educational Studies in Mathematics*, 29: 297–325.

Leung, F.K.S. (2005) Some characteristics of East Asian mathematics classrooms: based on data from the TIMSS 1999 video study. *Educational Studies in Mathematics*, 60(2): 199–215.

Lins, R., Rojano, T., Bell, A. and Sutherland, R. (2001) Approaches to algebra, in R. Sutherland, T. Rojano, A. Bell and R. Lins (eds) *Perspectives on School Algebra.* Amsterdam: Kluwer.

Mason, J. and Sutherland, R. (2002) *Key Aspects of Teaching Algebra in Schools.* London: QCA.

Mercer, N. (1995) *The Guided Construction of Knowledge: Talk Amongst Teachers and Learners.* Multilingual Matters: Clevedon.

Mesiti, C. and Clarke, D. (2003) Lesson patterns in superficially similar cultures: the USA and Australia. Paper presented as part of the symposium 'Perspectives on International Comparisons of Lesson Structure in Mathematics Classrooms in Germany, Japan, the USA, and Australia' at the 10th Biennial Conference of the European Association for Research on Learning and Instruction, Padova, Italy, 26–30 August.

Mills, S. (2004) Who's a Smartie? *Micromath*, 20(3): 17–23.

Mills, S., Sutherland, R. and Winter, J. (2005) *Numeracy: Interpreting Data.* TV programme for Teacher's TV, 1 March.

Misfeldt, M. (2005) Media in mathematical writing: can teaching learn from research practice? *For the Learning of Mathematics. An International Journal of Mathematics Education*, 25(2): 36–41.

Mok, I.A.C. (2003) The story of a 'teacher-dominating' lesson in Shanghai. Paper presented as part of the symposium 'Social Interaction and Learning in Mathematics Classrooms in Australia, Germany, Hong Kong, Japan, the Philippines, Sweden, and the United States' at the 10th Biennial Conference of the European Association for Research on Learning and Instruction, Padova, Italy, 26–30 August.

Moll, L. and Greenberg, J. (1992) Creating zones of possibilities: combining social contest for instruction, in L. Moll (ed.) *Vygotsky and Education*. Cambridge: Cambridge University Press.

Molyneux-Hodgson, S., Rojano, T., Sutherland, R. and Ursini, S. (2000) Mathematical modelling: the interaction of culture and practice. *Educational Studies in Mathematics*, 39: 167–83.

Noss, R. (1988) The computer as a cultural influence in mathematical learning. *Educational Studies in Mathematics*, 19(2): 251–68.

Nunes, T., Schliemann, A. and Carraher, D. (1993) *Street Mathematics and School Mathematics*. Cambridge: Cambridge University Press.

Nunes, T. and Bryant, P. (1996) *Children Doing Mathematics*. Oxford: Blackwell.

OFSTED (1993a) *Mathematics Key Stages 1, 2 and 3*. London: HMSO.

OFSTED (1993b) *The Teaching and Learning of Number in the Primary School*. HMSO: London.

Olivero, F. (2002) The proving process within a dynamic geometry environment. Unpublished PhD thesis, University of Bristol.

Olivero, F., John, P. and Sutherland, R. (2004) Seeing is believing: using *videopapers* to transform teachers' professional knowledge and practice. *Cambridge Journal of Education*, 34(2): 169–76.

Osborn, M. (1998) Being a pupil in England and France: findings from a comparative study, in A.M. Kazamias (ed.) *Education and the Structuring of the European Space*. Athens: Seirios Editions.

Papert, S. (1980) *Mindstorms: Children, Computers and Powerful Ideas*. Brighton: Harvester Press

Pea, R.D. (1993) Practices of distributed intelligence and designs for education, in G. Salomon (ed.) *Distributed Cognition*. Cambridge: Cambridge University Press.

Pepin, B. and Haggarty, L. (2002) Making connections and seeking links: 'Directed Numbers' in English, French and German textbooks. Paper presented at BERA conference, Exeter, September.

Perkins, D. (1993) Person-plus: a distributed view of thinking and learning, in G. Salomon (ed.) *Distributed Cognitions*. Cambridge: Cambridge University Press.

Popper, K. and Bennett, L. (1992) *In Search of a Better World: Lectures and Essays from Thirty Years*. London: Routledge.

Reynolds, D. and Muijs, D. (1999) Numeracy matters: contemporary policy issues in the teaching of mathematics, in I. Thompson (ed.) *Issues in Teaching Numeracy in Primary Schools*. Buckingham: Open University Press.

Rojano, T. (1996) Developing algebraic aspects of problem solving within a spreadsheet environment, in N. Bednarz, C. Kieran and L. Lee (eds) *Approaches to Algebra: Perspectives for Research and Teaching*. Dordrecht: Kluwer.

Rojano, T. and Sutherland, R. (1993) Towards an algebraic approach: the role of spreadsheets. *Proceedings of the XVII International PME Conference*, Japan.

Rojano, T., Sutherland, R., Ursini, S., Molyneux, S. and Jinich, E. (1996) Ways of solving algebra problems: the influence of school culture, *Proceedings of the 20th Conference of the International Group for the Psychology of Mathematics*, Valencia, Spain.

Royal Society/JMC (1997) *Teaching and Learning Algebra Pre-19* (1997) Report of a Royal Society/Joint Mathematical Council Working Group, Royal Society, Carlton House Terrace, London.

Salomon, G. (1993) *Distributed Cognitions, Psychological and Educational Considerations*. Cambridge: Cambridge University Press.

Schmidt, W.H., McNight, C., Valverde, G., Houang, R. and Wiley, D. (1997) *Many Visions, Many Aims, Volume 1: A Cross National Investigation of Curricular Intentions in School Mathematics*, Kluwer: Dordrecht.

Schmitlau, J. (2003) Cultural-historical theory and mathematics education, in A. Kazulin, B. Gindis, V. Ageyev and S. Miller (eds) *Vygotsky's Educational Theory in Cultural Context*. Cambridge: Cambridge University Press.

Scribner, S. and Cole, M. (1981) *The Psychology of Literacy*. Cambridge, MA: Harvard University Press.

Steiner, J.V. and Mahn, H. (1996) Sociocultural approaches to learning and development: a Vygotskian framework. *Educational Psychologist*, 31(3/4): 191–206.

Stigler, J. and Hiebert, J. (1997) Understanding and improving classroom mathematics instruction: an overview of the TIMSS video study. *Phi Delta Kappan*, September: 14–21.

Sutherland, R. (1984) A Pilot Logo course for 16–18 year old students, in E. Ramsden (ed.) *Microcomputers in Education 2*. Chichester: Ellis Horwood.

Sutherland, R. (1990) The changing role of algebra in school mathematics: the potential of computer-based environments, in P. Dowling and R. Noss (eds) *Mathematics Versus the National Curriculum*. London: The Falmer Press.

Sutherland, R. (1992) What is algebraic about programming in Logo?, in C. Hoyles and R. Noss (eds) *Logo and Mathematics: Research and Curriculum Issues*. Cambridge, MA: MIT Press.

Sutherland, R. (1993a) Connecting theory and practice: results from the teaching of Logo. *Educational Studies in Mathematics*, 24: 1–19.

Sutherland, R. (1993b) Symbolising through spreadsheets, *Micromath*, 8(4): 20–2.

Sutherland, R. (1994) The role of programming: towards experimental mathematics, in R. Biehler, R. Scholz, R. Strasser and B. Winkelman (eds) *Didactics of Mathematics as a Scientific Discipline*. Amsterdam: Kluwer.

Sutherland, R. (2002) *A Comparative Study of Algebra Curricula*. London: QCA.

Sutherland, R. and Balacheff, N. (1999) Didactical complexity of computational environments for the learning of mathematics. *International Journal of Computers for Mathematical Learning*, 4: 1–26.

Sutherland, R. and Rojano, T. (1993) A spreadsheet approach to solving algebra problems. *Journal of Mathematical Behaviour*, 12(4): 351–83.

Sutherland, R., Armstrong, V., Barnes, S., Brawn, R., Gall, M., Matthewman, S., Olivero, F., Taylor, A., Triggs, P., Wishart, J. and John, P. (2004) Transforming teaching and learning: embedding ICT into every-day classroom practices. *Journal of Computer Assisted Learning*, 20(6): 413–25.

Sutherland, R., Claxton, G. and Pollard, A. (eds) (2003) *Teaching and Learning Where Worldviews Meet*. Stoke-on-Trent: Trentham Books.

Sutherland, R., Howell, D. and Wolf, A. (1996) *A Spreadsheet Approach to Maths for GNVQ Engineering*. London: Hodder Headline.

Sutherland, R., Hoyles, C. and Noss, R. (1991) *The Microworlds Course: Description and Evaluation*. Final Report of the Microworlds Project, Volume 1, Institute of Education, University of London.

Sutherland, R., Olivero, F. and Weeden, M. (2004) Orchestrating mathematical proof through the UK of digital tools, in M.J. Hoines and A.B. Fuglestad (eds) *Proceedings of PME 28*. Bergen.

Sutherland, R., Robertson, S. and John, P. (2005) *InterActive Education: Teaching and Learning in the Information Age*. Report of a four-year research and development project funded from December 2000 until August 2004 by the UK Economic and Social Research Council.

Sutherland, R., Robertson, S. and John, P. (2007) *Improving Classroom Learning with ICT*. London: Routledge.

Sutherland, R., Rojano, T., Bell, A. and Lins, R. (eds) (2000) *Perspectives on School Algebra*. Amsterdam: Kluwer.

The New London Group (1996) A pedagogy of multiliteracies: designing social futures. *Harvard Education Review*, 66: 60–92.

Tomasello, M., Kruge, A. and Ratner, I. (1993) Cultural learning. *Behavioral and Brain Sciences*, 16: 450–88.

Triggs, P. and John, P. (2004) From transaction to transformation: ICT, professional development and the formation of communities of practice. *Journal of Computer Assisted Learning*, 20(6): 426–39.

Triggs, P., Barnes, S. and Sutherland, R. (2003) *Final Report for the NGfL Pathfinders Evaluation of the Impact on Standards and Institutional Effectiveness in the Pathfinder LEA*. Available at: http://becta.org.uk.

van Hiele, P.M. (1959/1985) The child's thought and geometry, in D. Fuys, D. Geddes and R. Tischler (eds) *English Translation of Selected Writings of Dina van Hiele-Geldorf and Pierre van Hiele*. Brooklyn, NY: Brooklyn College School of Education.

Vergnaud, G. (1990) Problem-solving and concept formation in the learning of mathematics, in H. Mandl et al. (eds) *Learning and Instruction*. London: Pergamon Press.

Vile, A. (1996) Development semiotics: the evolution of a theoretical framework for the description of meaning-making in mathematics education and mathematics. Unpublished PhD dissertation, South Bank University.

Von Glaserfield, E. (2003) Questions and answers about radical constructivism, in K. Tobis (ed.) *The Practice of Constructivism in Science Education*. Hillsdale, NJ: Lawrence Erlbaum.

Vygotsky, L.S. (1978) *Mind in Society: The Development of Higher Psychological Processes*. Cambridge, MA: Harvard University Press.

Vygotsky, L.S. (1994) The Problem of the Environment, in Val der Veer, R. & Valsiner, J. (ed) *The Vygotsky Reader*, Oxford: Blackwell.

Weeden, M. (2002) Proof, proof and more proof, *Micromath*, Autumn: 29–32.

Wertsch, J. (ed.) (1985) *Culture, Communication and Cognition*. Cambridge: Cambridge University Press.

Wertsch, J. (1991) *Voices of the Mind: A Sociocultural Approach to Mediated Action*. Hemel Hempstead: Harvester Wheatsheaf.

Wertsch, J. (1998) *Mind as Action*. Oxford: Oxford University Press.

Wertsch, J. and Stone, C.A. (1985) The concept of internalisation in Vygotsky's account of the genesis of higher mental functions, in Wertsch, J. (ed) *Culture, Communication and Cognition*. Cambridge: Cambridge University Press.

Wertsch, J.V. and Sohmer, R. (1995) Vygotsky on learning and development, in D. Kuhn (ed.) *Development and Learning: Reconceptualizing the Intersection*. Basel: Karger.

Winter, J., Salway, L., Ching Yee, W. and Hughes, M. (2004) Linking home and school mathematics: the home school knowledge exchange project, in O. Mcnamara and R. Barwell (eds) *Research in Mathematics Education Volume 6, Papers of the British Society for Research into Learning Mathematics*, London.

Zack, V. and Reid, D. (2000) A proof ought to explain: a classroom teacher-researcher, a mathematics educator and three cohorts of fifth graders seek to make meaning of a non-obvious algebraic expression. Proceeding of Canadian Mathematics Education Study Group.

Index

LANGUAGE FOR LEARNING MATHEMATICS
Assessment for Learning in Practice

Clare Lee

Assessment for learning is a powerful way to raise standards and improve learning. However, as this book shows, effective assessment for learning in the mathematics classroom depends on pupils being able and willing to use mathematical language to express their ideas. When discussion, negotiation and explanation are encouraged, teachers use assessment for learning creatively, the work quickly becomes more challenging and the pupils come to see themselves as successful learners.

Many pupils find it difficult to express ideas in mathematics because of problems with the language that is used to convey mathematical concepts. This book shows teachers how to help pupils express what they really know and understand, so that assessment for learning can be used. The book:

- Discusses what mathematical language is, and what it is not

- Suggests practical approaches to introducing more discourse into the classroom

- Explores the ideas of assessment for learning – rich questioning and dialogue, effective feedback, and peer and self assessment – and suggests how these can be used effectively in mathematics classrooms to improve learning

Language for Learning Mathematics is key reading for teachers and trainee teachers in mathematics, as well as assessment advisors at LAs.

Contents: *Acknowledgements - How this book tells its story - Increase discourse – increase learning - Mathematical language – what it is and what is isn't - Starting to talk in the mathematical classroom - Assessment for learning - Going further with purposeful communication in mathematics - The source of the ideas – delving into theory - Looking at practice more deeply - References - Index.*

2006   136pp   0 335 21988 8 Paperback   0 335 21989 6 Hardback

RAISING ACHIEVEMENT IN SECONDARY MATHEMATICS

Anne Watson

This book brings together research and professional knowledge to enhance the teaching of lower attaining students in secondary mathematics. Attainment in mathematics is an important social issue, since under-achievement can make a difference to future life choices, particularly amongst certain groups of students.

Raising Achievement in Secondary Mathematics shows how well-meant teaching strategies and approaches can in practice exacerbate underachievement in maths by making inappropriate demands on learners. As well as criticizing some of the teaching and grouping practices that are considered normal in many schools, the book also offers an alternative view of attainment and capability, based on real classroom incidents in which 'low attaining students' show themselves to be able to think about mathematics in quite sophisticated ways.

The author argues that teaching could be based on learners' proficiency, rather than on correcting deficits in knowledge and behaviour. She describes how a group of teachers who believed that their students could do better with higher expectations developed a range of principles and strategies to support their work – the students showed significant progress and the teachers felt they were doing a better job.

With numerous case studies, ideas and teaching strategies, this book is for anyone who is teaching, or learning to teach, mathematics.

Contents: *Acknowledgments - Learning about school mathematics - Abilities and understanding - Teachers' judgments - The impact of differences in practice and belief - The fallacy of 'getting to know' learners - Thinking mathematically in low-attaining groups - Approaches to reconstruction: test cramming versus developing proficiency - Identifying deep progress - Construction, reconstruction and renewal - References - Author index - contents index.*

2006   208pp   0 335 21860 1 Paperback   0 335 21861 x Hardback

CHILDREN'S MATHEMATICS 4-15
Learning from Errors and Misconceptions

Julie Ryan and Julian Williams

The mistakes children make in mathematics are usually not just 'mistakes' - they are often intelligent generalizations from previous learning. Following several decades of academic study of such mistakes, the phrase 'errors and misconceptions' has recently entered the vocabulary of mathematics teacher education and has become prominent in the curriculum for initial teacher education.

The popular view of children's errors and misconceptions is that they should be *corrected* as soon as possible. The authors contest this, perceiving them as potential windows into children's mathematics. Errors may diagnose significant ways of thinking and stages in learning that highlight important opportunities for new learning.

This book uses extensive, original data from the authors' own research on children's performance, errors and misconceptions across the mathematics curriculum. It progressively develops concepts for teachers to use in organizing their understanding and knowledge of children's mathematics, offers practical guidance for classroom teaching and concluded with theoretical accounts of learning and teaching.

Children's Mathematics 4-15 is a groundbreaking book, which transforms research on diagnostic errors into knowledge for teaching, teacher education and research on teaching. It is essential reading for teachers, students on undergraduate teacher training courses and graduate and PGCE mathematics teacher trainees, as well as teacher educators and researchers.

Contents: *Errors and misconceptions: what do they mean? - Children's mathematics: learning from errors and misconceptions - Mathematical discussions with children - Number and algebra - Shape and space - Measures and measurement - Probability and data handling - How children learn mathematics - Mathematics teaching - The research base*

2007   216pp   0 335 22042 8 Paperback   0 335 22043 6 Hardback